EFFECTIVE BOARD PARTICIPATION

James E. Seitz

Founding President, Retired
Edison State Community College

UNIVERSITY
PRESS OF
AMERICA

Lanham • New York • London

Library of Congress Cataloging-in-Publication Data

Seitz, James E.
Effective board participation / James E. Seitz.
p.   cm.
Includes index.
1. School board members – United States.   2. School boards – United
States.   I. Title.
LB2831.S45   1993   379.1'531'0973—dc20   93–39964 CIP

ISBN 0–8191–9371–2 (cloth : alk. paper)
ISBN 0–8191–9372–0 (pbk. : alk. paper)

Contents

Preface

The mark of the educated person, one may aver, is an ability to guess correctly. Although seemingly facetious, the remark harbors an element of profound, though humbling, truth. Anyone in a position of authority necessarily deals with an uncertain future when determining a course of action to satisfy a particular interest. Customarily, the best to be offered when choosing among alternatives is an educated guess. Therein lies the essence of sound decision making. The better informed the person the better are likely to be the plans, the predictions, the choices—the guesses.

All boards of education and trustees need "educated" people. Institutional welfare is too important to place in the hands of the ill-informed. Generally, persons serving on school, college, and university boards have accepted decision-making responsibilities that require knowledge which many do not have. Then, too, many have no guide or model available to follow. That they continue in the office while so poorly prepared for it is not a great surprise. Board members are seldom thoroughly screened before being seated in a policy-determining group, and some remain completely unaware of the unique preparation and skills needed for effectively directing the institution once elected or appointed.

This book could help alleviate the problems. It points up those aspects of conduct and performance which apply universally to members of all boards, regardless of types and levels of educational institutions involved. It can be used primarily as a source of information for members individually and in a planned program for the full board. Consultants, college presidents, and superintendents of schools will also find the topics to be useful in a board's annual retreat, in orientation conferences with new members, and for their own edification and reference. Experience indicates that general knowledge of the material presented in this work can lead to greater and better productivity in the performance of an important civic duty.

The topics covered will prove to be as helpful for certain conscientious members of long experience as for newly appointed or elected individuals. In addition to complete evaluation instruments, included are topics giving specific suggestions on preparing for participation, avoiding common traps, and becoming a sound performer in board affairs. Perhaps most important among the subjects covered is how to keep the institution moving forward by identifying and capitalizing on the institution's strengths. Anyone who has been considerate enough to accept a place on a board will undoubtedly encounter, with a little experience, many if not most of the problems and issues addressed.

Board members usually exhibit a conscientious attitude and willingness to learn, but they are busy people. They need a succinct, easy-to-read, no-nonsense manual which they may keep, take home, and refer to on occasion. It is the intent of this manual to provide that manner of orientation to the responsibilities.

For the most part the recommendations presented herein are experientially based, having been drawn from my many years of study and employment in educational administration. Firsthand observations, numerous discussions with educators and board members, and published reports of board action and behavior have had a major part in shaping that experience. Much of the material presented has been tested in practice—in my own retreats with boards and by distributing copies of sections to newly seated members. It should be just as beneficial in other situations.

James S. Seitz, Ph.D.

Chapter 1

Being a Board Member

Every board member deserves to be complimented. Membership on a board of control occurs because someone has, perhaps many people have, recognized in the individual certain qualities of leadership. Appointment or election to the office is unquestionably a high honor, and it is one which carries with it great responsibility.

Recognizing the Challenge

But being a board member isn't easy. That statement is definitely more factual than facetious for members of educational boards. As representatives of the people, board members are often held in critical review and assessment—sometimes by the press, occasionally by fellow associates, and frequently by the man on the street. Observers commonly expect board officials to perform with great wisdom, astute leadership, unrelenting devotion, and impeccable character. The expectations abound, with precious few "thanks" for the effort.

Being a board member *is* and honor, but it is not honorary. There are important obligations to be met in the office. First of all, a board official will usually have to spend many hours learning what it is all about. He or she is expected to devote evenings or other free time to reading minutes and relevant literature, to represent the board intelligently and consistently in the community, and to demonstrate unwavering allegiance by attending various functions held at the school or college with which affiliated. Anyone who accepts appointment or election to a board must also be resigned to attending occasionally long meetings, be regular in attendance, be prompt, be willing to engage in deliberations (sometimes lengthy and distressing ones), and generally be willing to work without remuneration or for scarcely enough money to cover incidental expenses. The seriousness of the demand becomes even more apparent once called upon to break away from important personal or professional duties.

By and large, members are held to a higher standard of performance than generally prevails among the public. Impeccable decorum in performance is one of these. In addition, there are important legal and extralegal aspects about the conduct of office to which serious attention must be directed. Among these are concerns about ethics and conflict of interest. Many challenges, indeed, become evident *vis-a-vis* the appointment or election, but probably the greatest requirement of all is to perform effectively throughout the entire term of office.

One's financial well-being can directly impact performance over the long term. Certainly, serving on a public, private, or proprietary educational board does not require great personal wealth—except, perhaps, on that private college board where appointees are expected to apply the monetary rule: give, get it, or get off. On the other hand, board service does not ordinarily pay enough to be considered a second income. The usual basic need is for each member to be unencumbered by stress and worry about paying bills or the demands of holding a moonlighting job to make ends meet.

The observer of numerous educational policies will note that several general, though widely divergent, practices exist regarding remunerating board members. The range of compensation may extend anywhere from nothing by a parochial school to $1,000 or more for attending a single quarterly meeting for a proprietary school. School and college board members in the public sector are ordinarily paid expenses for traveling to and from meetings, or they may receive a flat fee for each monthly meeting attended. Compensation of about twenty-five cents for each mile driven, fixed fees of forty to eighty dollars a meeting, and full payment for expenses incurred when attending an occasional, approved conference are common. Frequently, too, boards vote to return a large part of their pay to some fund, such as a scholarship or athletic fund, and individuals sometimes opt not to accept payment in any amount. With the exception of boards constituted primarily for show, as is true of some proprietary types, the commitment in time alone often far exceeds any monetary benefit to be gained from such service.

While the demands of board service are many, and the rewards few, a conscientious member can derive considerable personal satisfaction from the experience. An opportunity to exercise profound influence over a major institution in the community or region it serves can be highly motivational. A participant may, quite rightfully, recognize him- or herself as one among a select group who can leave an exemplary mark in the performance of a civic duty. Besides, the potential for deriving keen enjoyment from the friendships and, possibly, the board meetings with their occasional signs of progress and moments of humor remains constantly present. The degree of satisfaction each person gains from the experience will undoubtedly correspond in nature and extent to the effort put into it.

The dedicated member devotes considerable effort to meeting the challenges of membership. Theses four challenges are at the forefront of concern:

1. Knowing and properly observing board functions, duties, and relationships.

2. Knowing the nature of education and the unique character of the institution charged to represent.

3. Knowing the difference between policy making and administration.

4. Knowing how to assess, foster, and preserve institutional strength and quality.

New members of boards of control sometimes fail to reach their full potential in due time. Some do not recognize the need to isolate and cope with different thrusts, others lack the courage to undertake them, and still others accept the position strictly for purposes of self-aggrandizement and prestige. Such people can be expected to perform with impassive mediocrity or detrimental aplomb, despite their obligation to serve effectively.

Whatever the original motivation for seeking and accepting a seat on a board, the individual is duty bound to take an active interest in educational matters and be bent on seeing the school or college served excel. Anyone viewing the position as a civic responsibility, a means of putting something back into the community, or in another altruistic light is more likely to be prepared for service than others harboring more self-centered viewpoints. Not all have the qualities desired. It is in keeping with the diversity of humans that the average board is comprised of persons having mixed interests. Administrators and one or two of the more positively oriented board members can help improve the lot by passing literature about board conduct and responsibilities to those in need.

Having an Appropriate Attitude

Despite efforts to the contrary, boards seldom attain an ideal level of performance. Not often do all members of a group become fully cognizant either of the preparation necessary or of the functional perspective required for participating as expected. Of considerable importance in this regard are members' attitudes toward duties of the controlling board and purposes of the institution.

An extremely unfortunate problem with lay board membership is the occasional critic who gains office. Although the critic might not openly attempt to destroy the institution while seated on the board, an implicitly held recalcitrant motive can be just as counterproductive, however unbiased initial appearances may appear to be. The member-critic often proffers a receptive ear to hostile groups who have identified one of their kind through whom to channel vocal opposition. The true character of the serious critic eventually emerges, with vocal dissatisfaction and opposition happening in full view of students, faculty, and the public. Arguments will sometimes develop within the board, and occasionally a member or two will resign. Ironically, the resulting resignations will as often as not include an institution's most progressive leaders and supporters.

Counterproductive attitudes take many forms, although board minutes seldom record the instances of negative posture assumed by individual members. More than one chief administrator can recall the uneasy times while working with a member who overplayed the role of *devil's advocate.* Persons performing that role may oppose recommendations outright. They seem to search for weaknesses in proposals and seldom, if ever, recognize the strengths or merit of any recommendation but their own. The effect on the board, staff, and institution can be, in its extreme, demoralizing.

Do-it-my-way advocacy can be equally detrimental to staff morale and institutional progress. This role seems most likely to be exemplified by the business executives who expects the institution to be "run like" a corporation in the free enterprise sector. At other times, the role may be filled by the member who reveres a distant *alma mater* as the model of perfection to be emulated. One of these postures does not account for the different conditions and problems occurring within the business and educational fields, and the other fails to recognize differences existing among educational institutions of different size, control, location, funding, type, and objectives. Some principles of management do apply universally, but the strength of faculty and student self-determination and the ever-increasing regulation of schools and colleges through governmental control are important causative factors which lead to significant policy differences, including those existing in schools and colleges of the same type. The extent to which a board member relates to extraneous knowledge and expertise must, therefore, be appropriately tempered with knowledge of the context within it is to be applied.

A common mistake, particularly among newly appointed members, is a assumption of *having the answers*. This posture frequently characterizes those who have previously served on a board of control or have held employment in another educational system. Its persistent expression effectively deters efforts toward that person's enlightenment, total board involvement, and mutual respect. Even the authoritative role of the chief executive officer (the superintendent of schools or the president of the college) may be undermined in extreme instances.

Perhaps nothing can be more detrimental to relations between the chief executive and board than the presence of a member who is "out to get" the executive officer. A member so inclined might simply have a personal grudge to settle, a lasting memory of having applied for and been denied employment within the school system or college, or a need to prove to the other board members that they should have supported another choice for the chief executive's post at the outset.

Sitting in relative safety, adversative members have been known to work both openly and secretly to muster support among the full board and the public. One occurrence was observed wherein a member of a college board spear-headed a drive to oust the institution's president, because, as the member often said in public meetings, "a person in a top position is burned out after three years of doing the job and should be replaced." His constant carping on that point took its toll, causing the president to resign in his fourth year of service. The instigator in this scene was an architect who continued to operate as such after twenty-six years in business. His unfortunate and peculiar brand of logic became fully evident when he argued publicly that burn-out doesn't occur in his profession.

A variety of negative attitudes and motivations have been observed in practice. In many of those instances executive performance has been undermined, with open hostility and dissension eventually developing among the personalities involved. Little wonder that longevity among appointees to the chief administrative position has been only about five years on the average.

The very nature of board membership places individual idiosyncrasies and characteristics of personality in the public limelight, and expression of those traits can have an impact far more significant in that setting than would likely occur in private life. Dealing with rumor instead truth, supposition instead of fact, or opinion instead of logic are but a few of the observable pitfalls. Such expressions can be just as counterproductive as being unprepared for board meetings, looking for a scapegoat when results are not as expected, taking "cheap shots" at other members or staff, becoming a "yes man" for the chairperson or executive, "grinding and axe" for a special interest group, or using the position for personal gain and self-interest to the detriment of board functioning and institutional progress. The consequences of any one of these attitudes or actions can be far-reaching in an educational setting.

The possibilities for ineffective participation are about as numerous as the opportunities for human failure. The fields of psychology and ethics can be consulted for evidence of the many failings in behavior which befall individuals. Board members are not immune from those shortcomings. In recognition thereof, the conscientious member will carefully analyze the performance of others for purposes of improving ones's own.

Acknowledging Board Limitations

Boards of education and college trustees have inherent limitations. Very often new members join the policy-determining body with little if any previous experience in many of the important matters for which the body holds responsibility. Matters of extreme importance, such as finance, campus and building construction, personnel policies, student services, instruction, and the fundamental goals of the educational system may be completely foreign concerns. The newly seated member customarily comes aboard without ever before having hired or evaluated a chief executive, and some seem never to fully comprehend the effects of organized faculty demands on the process. Moreover, members do not benefit from a lengthy apprenticeship such as that experienced by many administrators as they work from teaching to mid-management to executive-level positions in the educational field. For that reason, the chances of ever observing a completely knowledgeable board are minimal.

Turnover aggravates the situation. Membership changes often, and the chair (a station from which sound leadership is expected) usually rotates even more often than length of term. Terms of office expire just when the incumbents become most informed. The demands and responsibilities of the board persist all the while new members and officers concentrate on learning their roles.

Although arguments have been advanced for improving the manner of determining board membership, the purpose at hand is not to call for a change in the usual methods of forming and organizing such controlling groups. On the contrary, the object is to accept practices as they are, focus on the problems inherent in the different systems, and suggest some tried and tested methods which will help boards and members perform their duties most effectively. How a board discharges its responsibilities is more relevant than how the membership has been determined. A willingness of the members to learn and perfect performance will have far more impact than limitations in method of identification, selection, and election or appointment.

Making the Commitment

Before accepting appointment or seeking election to a board, a prospect should determine what the expectations are and whether or not he or she can fulfill them. The aspirant might first review the law that established the institution in order to gain an understanding of the governing body's responsibilities. A second important step might be the reading of policies and bylaws regulating the board's conduct and institutional activities. Once the legal requirements and functional obligations are understood, attention can then be directed to an analysis of the personal qualities needed.

Personal qualities of notable variety are needed for productive board service. Included are intellectual skill, decision-making skill, social skill, political skill, and a functional skill of some kind. The individual's training and job skill may be an asset to board functioning. Some persons bring to the board a specialty of exceptional worth to the organization, enabling them to lend advice on matters of finance, building construction, personnel management, accounting, or other technical area.

Effective members further demonstrate capabilities of operating as ambassadors and intermediaries between the organization and the community when called upon. They also hold to a high level of ethical conduct. Despite the demands of office which often prevail, the best of them seem always to be able to maintain a priceless sense of humor.

An aspirant to a board should always question whether or not accepting membership will deny a place to a more qualified or more interested contestant. An affirmative answer would seem to suggest foregoing acceptance and better preparing for a future possibility. Does this seem too much to expect? Perhaps, but this can work. A capable chairperson can bring the matter to each aspirant's attention without creating embarrassment or feelings of ill will. In fact, private boards routinely interrogate all persons being considered for appointment, making certain they understand expectations attendant to the office.

Additional questions to be addressed before accepting board membership are:

1. Can I devote the time necessary for participating effectively?
2. Am I a good listener and not afraid to speak my mind?
3. For what appropriate reasons would I serve?
4. Can I be truly loyal to the institution and its mission?
5. Has the institution progressed soundly and with good reputation or is the potential for such there?
6. Can I support management and the policies being recommended?
7. Do I have the breadth of experience necessary to deal with the management of educational problems?
8. Do I have the personality and sophistication to cope with the assignment in a professional manner?

Board members must subordinate personal interests to those of the institution. That stance is essential. The fiduciary relationship in board affairs hold members to a standard of good faith and honesty in their actions. Persons reluctant to comply with that standard should seek another pastime.

A sense of commitment to the institution is an extremely important requirement. Before assuming office, a prospective board member should engage in serious introspection regarding feelings toward the school's mission. One who cannot accept and unhesitatingly support that mission probably will not work most constructively toward fulfilling major goals and objectives, nor will one who had bitterly led opposition against creating a school or the passing of a tax levy readily try to work for its furtherance. While in office such a person can engage ever so subtly, or too crudely, in the condemnation of important administrative and institutional efforts.

The men and women who serve on a board basically determine the quality of that board's performance, assuming all organizational aspects are in good order. Unlike members of boards in the corporate sector who are selected on a standard of fifteen or more years of top management experience, members of educational boards are often selected on the basis of assumed potential. Relevant experience becomes a secondary consideration. Commonly, members are chosen to reward them in connection with matters only loosely related to education. Many, of course, are there because of the leadership qualities they have been perceived to possess.

Board membership at any level of education is most assuredly a unique function in our society. Experience in other occupations helps develop qualities that are desirable, but no one comes to a board for the first time prepared to be the ideal member. Limited knowledge and dysfunctional attitudes are the common problems. All members need special preparation, both in a beginner's orientation and later to keep abreast the complex issues of the profession. A basic requirement for service on an educational board, therefore, is a commitment to strive for increased knowledge and competence in boardmanship.

Preparing for Effective Participation

How, in the presence of limitations resulting from rotating membership, inexperienced participants, and frequently changing leadership, can a board discharge its duties effectively on a continuing basis? There are several workable approaches: (1) The board can collectively address the issue and organize for ongoing self-edification, (2) a consultant or the chief executive officer can be called upon periodically to provide in-service education, and (3) each new member can be given intensive orientation by members of the board and administration. A combination of these methods may be preferred in a particular situation.

Every board member has a personal responsibility to prepare for the duty. A common error of assumption is that appointment or election to a board implies qualification and preparedness for it. There is a propensity to recognize neither personal nor board limitations.

Despite the customary limitations, recognizing obligations and constantly striving to fulfill them are basic requirements. The need to maintain institutional progress in an era of tight budgets, criticism about low standards, and failure of today's graduates to measure up presents a challenge that should not be taken lightly. A member cannot help direct the institution on a positive course by serving passively.

Fortunately, most conditions and qualifications can be improved upon, and recognition of that fact becomes necessary if meaningful improvement is likely to occur. Members and entire boards should remain aware. Topics to help them prepare individually and collectively for discharging duties effectively are presented in the remaining chapters of this book.

Chapter 2

Measuring Up to the Responsibility

A board member sits in trust. The very act of appointing or electing an individual to a position of control over an educational institution carries with it expectations about that person's integrity, ability, and trustworthiness in office.

Although the word *trustee* has been applied in education to members of college and university boards, the term has meaning for boards of control of all kinds. It signifies responsibility for managing property or for overseeing the administration of something for others. That, for members of school and college boards, means the welfare of the institution is vested in a few people for the benefit of many. Responsibility for the progress and well-being of the institution resides with the board as a whole, and for every action taken the board remains accountable to the taxpayers or other citizens who have legal and moral interests in the institution.

For the novice, especially one who has not previously served on a board nor been trained for it, realization of the importance and magnitude of the responsibility can be unsettling. As a result, idle observation in place of active participation may occur during the initial period of learning and socialization. Only in time can the newcomer be expected to discharge duties of the office effectively.

Devoting the Time

Board members can contribute responsibly only by doing the things expected of them: attending meetings regularly, reading informational mailings, studying background material, performing special assignments, and participating in training sessions when called upon. In short, they must be willing to devote the time to do those things. A person planning to join a board should figure on spending about six to twelve hours a month on business, including a monthly board meeting that typically runs a couple of hours. Certain circumstances could make a big difference, however. Attendance at state or national conventions might increase the total time commitment considerably. Still other demands on time can be expected, such as training for duty on the board, carrying out a committee assignment on a sticky problem, or preparing a special report for delivery before the full board. Additionally, a beginner will probably have to devote extra time reading literature and consulting with staff in order to become acclimated and to gain the specialized knowledge needed.

Some duties are always highly demanding. Anyone who has ever held an office knows the feeling. Filling the position of presiding officer can be most demanding, but a minor office can also be very restrictive. A committee chairperson's or secretary's duties can easily take up several evenings or weekends that might otherwise be free. The need to set aside personal plans in order to carry out such assignments are among the expressions commonly heard at board meetings.

It is customary to schedule meetings of the full board regularly so that members can plan vacations and other personal activities accordingly. To aid in the process, many boards will not hold meetings during one or two months in the summer and the month of December, thereby avoiding periods when staff and members normally schedule vacations. When a conflict does arise, as is bound to occur on occasion, the member who misses a meeting is expected to do the work necessary to keep informed and remain abreast activities.

Despite the best laid plans, instances occur which place extraordinary demands on the members. Special meetings called to handle some unforeseen emergency, a day-long retreat for purposes of the members' enlightenment, and any of a variety of the other assignments previously mentioned can be expected during a term of office. Thus, the member whose daily schedule can be readily altered may have a distinct advantage over others relative to fulfilling obligations.

One of the greatest impediments to board functioning is absenteeism. An absentee loses touch with activities to some extent, a condition which could seriously detract from the board's functioning and progress. Attendance at ninety percent of all meetings is a reasonable expectation. Not only can a member's influence be severely limited by attending less often than that, but both board functioning and institutional progress can suffer if other members are also frequently absent. High rates of absenteeism have been know to result in a failure to achieve the quorum needed for taking official action on matters of pressing importance.

Learning the Business

The things to be learned in preparation for board service can be extensive. First, the member must develop an awareness of matters about board operation and policy determination, including applicability of the law to board and institutional responsibilities and how the board should function in matters of policy, personnel, student services, finances, facilities, curriculum, and extracurricular activities. Second to be gained is knowledge of the institution—its mission, philosophy, goals, purposes, organizational structure, history, and achievements. A need to be cognizant of trends in education which may affect the organization relates to this category of requirements. The third area pertains to evaluation, that is, learning how to evaluate institutional progress, board performance, and personal effectiveness. Concomitant with this is the mastery of the subtleties and intricacies of working with administrators and associates on personal and professional bases, albeit within full view and review of the public and the press.

As a minimum, every board member should be given a thorough orientation by the chief executive. The superintendent of schools or college president can provide policy manuals, copies of board minutes, bulletins and other documents which will serve as an initial introduction. The materials should be presented as soon as appointment or election to the board is known. The executive can also provide verbal instruction. These initial activities are important, but they are seldom enough. New board members usually need follow-up instruction, no matter that few ask for it.

When properly oriented, members are inclined to be receptive to additional instruction through an in-service program for the entire board. The program many be part of a regular annual session which, fundamentally, is devoted to the improvement of board functioning. Meetings of this type should be specially and solely scheduled for the purpose intended, and they should be attended by everyone as nearly as possible for the full time. Scheduling of the program should be, preferably, for one day.

Who will conduct the in-service sessions may depend on the quality of the relationships existing at the time. The chairperson and the chief administrator can develop the agenda and decide which one will perform leadership duties. Administrative staff might be asked to contribute to the program, although in some situations the services of a paid consultant will be most beneficial.

Presence at the training sessions is not enough, for the attendants must have a willingness and desire to learn. Members bring some expertise to the board, but the fact that one is expert in, say, finance is no excuse for that person not seeking knowledge in other areas of endeavor. Neither should members be content to rely completely on an expert's opinion or advice. They should be interested enough to become intelligently informed so that decisions are truly board made, rather than those of a single "expert."

Attaining a High Level of Participation

A person's worth on a board of control relates directly to the level of his or her participation. It is the depth of recommendations and comments that counts. In order words, intelligent expression in the decision-making process basically determines the effectiveness of participation. This relationship between depth of knowledge and sound decision-making becomes evident in the quality of the policies which emerge.

Board members must usually spend some time before being able to function at the highest level possible. With effort, education, and experience, an astute person can grow in knowledge, emerging from participation at the level of routine board activity, the lowest level, to the highest level of decision-making as its pertains to the institution in its social context.

The several levels of knowledge relative to the decision-making function are described, from low to high, as follows:

Level I: Knowledge of routine board procedures and activities—committee functions, bylaws, parliamentary procedure; legal requirements and restrictions; member duties and responsibilities; ethical and moral obligations; budget, facilities, staff appointments, etc.

Level II: Knowledge of the institution, its qualities and functions —organizational structure, historical development, and uniqueness of the institution; curriculum, students, staff, intramural activities, etc.; institutional strengths, weaknesses, progress, and problems; and special concerns, e.g., handling the press, financing, taxing, and accreditation.

Level III: Knowledge of the field of operation—history, legislation, trends, issues, developments, and special conditions such as faculty's role in governance in the particular field of education (public higher education, private education, etc.) and sub-field (community colleges, unified school districts, parochial high schools, etc.) as they impact on the functioning of the institution.

Level IV: Knowledge of relevant societal conditions—broad historical, judicial, political, legal, and social trends; national, regional, and local conditions or events; and other occurrences and probabilities which have affected or would likely affect education generally or the institution specifically.

The place of evaluation in the scheme may not be readily apparent. The process, whether concentrated on assessments of personnel or institutional performance, logically falls at *Level II*, but knowledge at all levels will likely lead to better understanding and action.

Also, the more knowledgeable each member becomes at each level the better able the assembly will be to do the planning, forecasting, and decision-making needed for future development. Boards ordinarily devote most of their time to routine recommendations. They should devote at least one-half of their meeting time to planning, long- and short-range.

Intelligent planning occurs where there is adequate knowledge of trends and conditions in the general field of operation. Board members do not always realize the need to be so informed. As a result, many of the decisions that relate to forecasting and planning a future course are based solely on executive and staff recommendations. This shortcoming is not totally bad, however, for the judgment of professionals should often prevail.

On the other hand, executives ordinarily welcome informed input. It is the uninformed opinion which causes the most difficulty. Administrators are naturally receptive to ideas when the uncertainties of prediction are involved. They will work diligently to develop a board-executive partnership when contemplating some imminent event, as, for example, when speculating about the probability and possible effects of a severe shortage and rationing of gasoline. Something similar can be said about modern-day woman's independence and movement away from housework. Once an important trend or condition has been identified, the future of the institution and alternate plans for it can be charted according to predictions of the differential effects. Plans for the university, community college, adult vocational school, private high school, or other educational enterprise the board is charged to direct can be set accordingly. The greater the array of informed judgment in such analyses the better are likely to be the predictions and plans for the future.

Understanding the Educational Enterprise

Educational organizations are characterized by conditions not immediately apparent to all laymen and women. For one thing, a diffusion of power occurs within public schools and to a greater extent within colleges and universities. The practice is without equal in proprietary schools and private companies. Faculty and other employees commonly demand to be involved in policy decisions, the likes of which remain the prerogative of top management in business and industry. Corporate executives who sit on school or college boards seem to have difficulty understanding that fact, and administrators' explanations of the historical development of faculty power may have little effect on the level of understanding. Nevertheless, this distribution of power influences various managerial positions. A stance of negotiation and compromise instead of imposed authority characterizes the decision-making process. Policies, therefore, must often be constructed in consultation with personnel within the organization who might be affected by the board's decisions.

A somewhat oversimplified, comparative model is presented in the accompanying diagram. It shows in a general way the differences in the division of power occurring in various organizations.

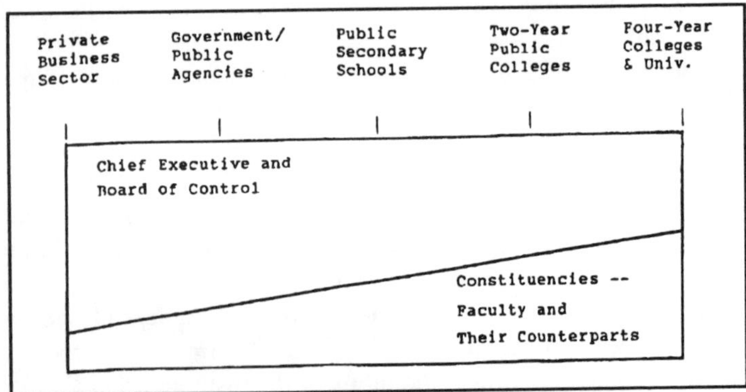

Figure 2.1 Focus of Decision Making

Wide distribution and diffusion of decision-making power within an organization increases internal bureaucracy. The effect on an organization already burdened by extensive governmental impositions can be tremendous. One important constraint is that projects must be assigned considerably more time for completion than generally holds in the private sector. A possible advantage is the wide base of support generated.

In addition to seeking power, faculty make strong demands for security, salary, and benefits unique to education. The public more and more frequently counters with demands for increased services without corresponding increases in support. This combination of demands and constraints sets schools and colleges apart from practically all other organizations. Competing conditions such as these must be understood by both board and management for the two to work harmoniously. Instances of open confrontation and stress, which the conditions occasionally cause, are particularly difficult to address in the absence of mutual understanding and agreement.

Knowing the Law

Another important area of understanding is the law. All boards operate under laws which regulate or limit their activities.

The legal requirements for public boards generally take several forms: those defining authority of the board as a whole, those regulating specific activities and defining responsibilities such as purchasing or disposing of property, and those specifying obligations of individual members relative to election procedures, financial disclosure, and conflict of interest. Further, there ordinarily exists an extensive body of regulations which pertain indirectly to boards, being directed primarily toward the actions and activities of staff, faculty and students, or other institutional matters.

Board members should be apprised of the legal restrictions and legislative enactments regulating their performance. Copies of applicable laws and regulations should be made available to each new member by the chief executive, with interpretative assistance provided by the board's legal counsel. Important among these are provisions on ethics which guard against possible conflict of interest and influence peddling by public officials. Regulations requiring public officials to file financial disclosure statements should also be presented to each person upon assuming office.

An equally significant area of required understanding pertains to the potent legal grounds accorded persons inclined toward litigation. In view of the board's potential exposure to charges of wrongdoing in dealing with personnel, the entire board should be aware of the fundamental guarantees accorded individuals through federal legislation and the U. S. Constitution. Student and faculty rights of due process consist of one of the crucial areas of understanding. The right of the aggrieved to a fair and unbiased hearing without fear of reprisal, to be represented by counsel, and to confront witnesses are several aspects of the process which must be carefully observed. Legal entanglements can surely arise where such guarantees are not provided. The need to follow written rules and policies without neglect or violation, the need to base personnel decisions on all relevant facts, and the need to avoid special or preferential treatment consist of other essential considerations. Consultation with competent counsel when considering matters involving personnel should occur, insofar as possible, before some action is taken.

Besides the legal concerns mentioned, laws defining general authority and duties of the board should be copied and distributed to the members. These might be made part of a board manual and should be given due consideration during the annual training session. An alert executive will also try to keep the board unformed of new and impending legislation, but only that information which is pertinent and not voluminous should be mailed out.

Keeping Informed

In the area of public education, the preponderance of legislation and regulations impinging upon the schools and colleges from state and federal sources can be overwhelming. New laws seem to continue to emerge in unrelenting fashion. Rules and regulatory restrictions, too, are being produced prolifically by agencies of government. The amount of time these new laws, regulations, and statutory amendments must be given can be excessively demanding of the chief executive, especially when pressing institutional affairs need immediate attention. So that nothing of importance goes unnoticed, board members should also remain alert for notices about legal matters published in literature at their disposal. Details of litigation in sexual harassment cases constitute a relevant example.

The services of an attorney to study and report on impending and newly enacted legislation can be helpful. The responsible person might report periodically at regular meetings, with review and screening by the chief executive occurring beforehand. In that way, the executive officer exercises preliminary control over the presentation in terms of its length, importance, and timeliness.

A board's most fundamental need is to remain informed about internal matters. The chief executive officer is responsible for presenting information about developments impending within the educational enterprise. The board member's obligation is to solicit and attempt to understand as much information as needed for making intelligent decisions.

Exerting Influence

Every board member, whether elected or appointed, is duty-bound to work positively for the betterment of the organization charged to represent. To do that each must make his or her presence felt in meetings, particularly during deliberations resulting in institutional policy. The individual must not only be informed about and show interest in any subject presented but also be prepared to debate the pros and cons of the issue under discussion. For the sake of appearances, acceptance, and effectiveness, discussions and commentary on a subject should always occur before, not after, a vote is recorded.

Next to performing in regular meetings, committee assignments offer good possibilities for exemplary performance. Board chairmen and chairwomen sometimes establish committees to meet with administrators over some particular detail or proposal—all the while holding out great expectations for the appointees to gain appreciably by participating. Unfortunately, results do not always measure up to expectations. Being out of direct view of the full board and the public, some members will take the assignment casually or even show complete boredom during meetings of their committee. Their participation is virtually nil. While such extreme behaviors might be rare, an alert chairperson will make an effort to appoint at least one member who can be expected to remain conscientious and provide intelligent input to the group.

The community is another place for exerting influence. Board members are often more favorably positioned for that than employees of the institution. A board member remains part of the constituency of the community and, by virtue of position, gains recognition as an authoritative representative. That person can be an asset without a parallel, specifically when making statements privately and publicly which are supportive of the school or college. The position can also be +used to advantage in fund-raising drives or by obtaining gifts for the institution. Not all members generate the support that they might. Some, in fact, fail to defend the institution and staff in instances of unfounded criticism, and, occasionally, one will make statements detrimental to the institution's cause. The effect, in any case, can be considerable.

Third in the list of important areas of an individual member's realm of influence is the legislature and other controlling bodies at the state level. Using the position as board official to express views on legislation or regulations which impinge upon the local operation is expected and usually desired by members of governmental bodies. An occasional letter or luncheon meeting can serve as the means for advancing the board's preferences.

Congressional representatives are among those to be contacted. Acting collectively or individually, board members can exert their influence for the benefit of both institution and education. Carefully designed strategies should be developed to avoid overlooking appropriate opportunities. Above all, board members must have the stature to recognize when to call upon a legislator, including one of the opposing party or political belief. To reject as commencement speaker, for example, an influential legislator because that person holds political views different from those of an influential member of the board seems woefully shortsighted. Partisan politics and party loyalty have a place in our democratic scheme, but that place is not above the welfare of the educational entity which the board member has agreed to serve.

Using an Association

An association can be a major source of legislative information, especially as regards significant, impending legislation. Several state and national associations keep their membership informed of such legislation, and they frequently espouse an official position about it.

Legislative updating is not the only service offered, by any means. Associations commonly offer services designed to educate members to their many responsibilities. The publications, conventions, and conferences are often an excellent means of keeping boards apprised of current thought and practice, and some associations provide a lobbying function or vehicle by which preferences on important subjects can be expressed to legislators. Some offer still other services, including liability insurance, orientation seminars or workshops, criteria for evaluating board performance, executive search services, and consultation on collective bargaining, board-executive relations, affirmative action, and many other helpful topics. An extensive variety of beneficial services are usually made available.

The selection of an association not only should occur but it should occur after careful consideration. Here, again, the chief administrative officer can give direction. He or she can identify active state and national organization's, as well as summarize for the board information relative to fees for joining, goals of the association, and services offered. Finally, a recommendation might be made about which association seems most likely to extend the services desired in light of local needs.

Several well-known national associations solicit membership for full board affiliation. Some accept individual memberships. Those listed below have gained extensive recognition within their respective constituent groups.

> Association of Community College Trustees
> 1740 N Street, N.W.
> Washington, DC 20036
>
> Association of Governing Boards of Universities and Colleges
> One Dupont Circle, N.W., Suite 400
> Washington, DC 20036
>
> National Association of Boards of Education
> National Catholic Education Association
> 1077 30th Street, N.W., Suite 100
> Washington, DC 20007
>
> National School Boards Association
> 1680 Duke Street
> Alexandria, VA 22314

Once affiliated, it is the responsibility of members of the board to participate actively. They can be expected, within reason, to read the literature distributed, attend conferences, and offer input to the association through writing, speaking, or voting. If none of the individuals who comprise a board are committed to an active role, other than incidental learning from the association's literature, there is good reason to question whether or not institutional dollars should be spent for the privilege.

Making One's Presence Count

Having learned what the institution is about, studied the legal requirements, and made an effort to remain abreast developments in the field, a board member has another important personal obligation to fulfill: the knowledge gained must be put to use. A member contributes little by sitting back passively at meetings without entering the discussions and deliberations. A passive member may be an intelligent voter, but that person seldom influences decisions of the full board.

The biggest problem for some new members is a reluctance to discuss matters openly, leaving decisions and deliberations to the more experienced (and presumably more knowledgeable) persons in the group. Such reluctance is not uncommon. It may occur out of courtesy or deference to others, or it may be the manifestation of sheer reticence. It can be a potent deterrent to complete participation and board vitality. Of course, some members do participate effectively from the time they first join the board. Of those who do, more often than not they enter meetings well prepared. They have, as a minimum, thoroughly read the material mailed to them prior to each meeting.

A high level of influence distinguishes the effective member. Experience indicates that board members need not be vociferous, eloquent, or profuse, but the influential ones do speak intelligently. They have acquired essential knowledge before open discussion on a proposal or issue begins.

Effective participants are cognizant of the need to listen and to offer conclusions only when sure of their efficacy. Colleagues readily judge their peers. Hastily made, ill-informed opinions do little to instill feelings of confidence among the group.

When no clear-cut conclusion can be drawn and no decision reached beforehand, an adequately prepared member will have thought through several pertinent questions to elicit from administrators the information needed for arriving at an informed recommendation. This practice of questioning has considerable merit. It is by far preferable to the spurious action of calling for action on a motion before the main idea has been properly discussed and understood by everyone concerned. The French philosopher Voltaire left little more to be contemplated on this score when he beckoned us to "judge a man by his questions rather than by his answers."

Being A Creative Participant

While becoming an effective participant has never been a simple task, being a creative one presents even greater challenges. Open meetings seldom provide a forum most conducive to creative thought and expression. Administrators come prepared with set resolutions, backed by supporting data and a staff charged to advanced their ideas. The board has very little left to do but vote. This practice is not totally undesirable, for no one should tolerate an executive who lacks decisiveness and seems unable to defend administrative proposals. An executive officer is expected to show leadership. The danger is that the board will be fed foregone conclusions as long as the majority continue to apply the "rubber stamp" of approval.

The general lack of creative work during board meetings has not been the result of executive influence alone, however. Presiding officers have also played a substantial part by allowing agenda to be filled with routine matters of budget, buildings, and personnel, by controlling meetings in the manner of an assembly line, and by assigning committees to work on developmental concerns beyond the view of the full board. Members, too, have shared the responsibility. Instead of speculating in public, they have preferred to do their creative thinking in the safety and privacy of informal gatherings before and after regular board meetings.

Boards must now seek other ways of doing business. The advent of sunshine laws in many places has made that necessary. Those laws severely limit the topics that may be discussed behind closed doors.

A creative person will take an active part whenever possible. Although no effort will be made to discourage solid planning by executive and staff, through constructive suggestion a forward-thinking individual will insist on time being set aside for planning the future of the institution. Specifically suggested will be to schedule several meetings or parts of meetings for discussion by staff and board of the alternatives in future facilities development, instructional programming, funding, and any other aspect of institutional development of a policy nature. By this means, all members will be given an opportunity to apply their creative talents in the all-important area of planning.

Once the opportunity is provided, it then becomes each member's responsibility to be prepared to make an intelligent contribution. That contribution may be nothing more that a series of informed questions which, for many, is the best way to bring out new ideas.

Improving Individual Performance

The conscientious board member strives for excellence in performance. A desire to perform in an exemplary manner is the compelling ingredient, implicitly recognizing the importance of *planning* and *preparing* thoroughly for purposes of *participating* effectively.

Planning. Improvement in individual performance is most likely to result when a plan, a strategy, exists for achieving it. The process should involve establishing individual goals for learning about board responsibilities, and it should include the development of a time schedule, with an hour or two weekly set aside for concentrating on institutional affairs. The plan should also provide for periodic review and evaluation.

Preparing. As trite as the suggestion may seem, being prepared sets the stage for participating effectively. Preparation pertains to the ongoing learning of general information and of that which pertains specifically to meetings. Thorough preparation is important on both counts. A study of information which applies broadly to the school or college, general policy, applicable law, and other relevant concerns can be as important as having studied the minutes and topics under immediate consideration.

In addition to updating through activities such as in-service training and involvement in an association, each member should develop a habit of reading the literature distributed by the chief executive officer. Members should prepare further by giving thought to resolutions and topics in meeting agenda, and they should develop, as appropriate, possible alternative proposals or recommendations for consideration. An extensive variety of subjects might be brought under scrutiny in that way, including considerations of community involvement, legislative trends, board functioning, and extra-curricular activities, to name a few.

Participating. The effectiveness of a member can be determined by the individual's impact on legislation, community support, and board decisions for the betterment of the institution. A quantitative measure of performance is the frequency with which the member poses meaningful questions and has ideas accepted or adopted by the board. A qualitative measure is the positiveness of effect on the conduct of affairs.

A board member must take election or appointment to the office seriously. The conscientious person might look upon each meeting with associates as a means of improving the next one. Newly seated members, especially, might benefit by following that advice.

An individual's effectiveness can be markedly limited by being absent frequently and failing to do the homework. The progress of the board is hampered proportionately. If the member is inactive, uninterested, or simply ignorant of institutional practices, the institution is similarly affected.

Every board, every institution, needs people who strive to do their best. Observance of the suggestions presented in this chapter relative to attitude, planning, preparation, and creating an impact will prove helpful to anyone striving to achieve a commendable level of sophistication in governing an educational institution.

Chapter 3

Functioning As A Board

Because they set an example for the management of internal affairs, boards responsible for people-centered institutions ought to be held to high standards of performance. Order and efficiency are proper expectations. This does not imply that uncompromising rigidity must be adhered to in the conduct of business. Some flexibility, like occasional failure, is tolerable. Nonetheless, a board's effectiveness in planning and controlling institutional activities deserves close scrutiny.

For a full board to be effective, individual members must observe certain ground rules. Among these are the rules by which meetings are conducted, when and where not to speak for the board, how to have topics placed on agenda, when an executive session is permitted by law, how to evaluate performance, and a host of other practical considerations. Members must be made aware of individual responsibilities as explained in Chapter 2, and they should be instructed in board procedures if orderliness is to be attained and maintained. The open-minded person will be receptive to orientation in these matters, despite the constraints on his or her time.

Performing Duties

The duties of controlling boards have been the subject of many conferences, written articles, and certain legislation. In addition, some charters contain a list of duties. Many of the statements are rooted in tradition, and many permit considerable latitude in meeting the challenges.

Several commonly acknowledged duties are:

1. The selection and continual support of a chief executive officer.

2. The development, with the chief executive, of principal institutional goals and policies.

3. The development, ownership, and preservation of the institution's property and assets.

4. The adjudication of matters of governance and personnel in the role of court of appeals.

5. The assessment and maintenance of institutional progress, strength, and effectiveness.

6. The conduct of business for the benefit of constituent welfare.

7. The perpetuation of distinctive purposes for which the institution was established.

The preservation of institutional purposes and authority poses one of the gravest problems for boards. This necessitates resisting encroachment by external forces. Interference in the structure and usurpation of power by an agency of government is one sure way to diminish local autonomy. Equally important is resoluteness in maintaining vested authority in the face of pressures from special-interest groups in the community and within the institution.

The idea that a board must take into account the wishes of various constituencies has led to gross misunderstanding. True, a board should be concerned about different desires, but that does not mean the board should (if it could) implement each suggestion or request it receives. Boards run the risk of responding to individuals whom they believe to be broadly representative or extraordinarily influential, and those boards on which faculty and students hold membership must be especially on guard against confusing wants with needs. Peer pressures on faculty and student representatives can produce expressions entirely counter to larger interests. The proper response is to act in accordance with broadly based constituent interests and institutional purposes.

The requests and demands of some groups are not always easily dismissed, however. Consider the present-day clamor for teaching youngsters about gay and lesbian lifestyles, for instance. Any board directly confronted with that issue must decide if the obstreperous arguments for equal treatment of the minorities involved carries more credence than the opposing voice of those who say such material has no place in a required course of study. One thing is certain: The board could find itself on the firing line no matter which way it rules on this matter.

Whether serving public or private constituencies, board members must remain vigilant in holding to a perspective as broad as possible. They should never lose sight of the need to exercise judgment in a manner beneficial to all, or most, persons concerned. Board members have a fundamental obligation in that regard.

A board's role is pluralistic. In giving attention to what might be called *the general welfare*, the controlling body must be certain that learning will occur effectively and within the mission of the institution. It must also administer affairs in accordance with law, while protecting against statutory revisions and governmental regulations which might infringe on its authority. Maintaining a climate favorable for executive leadership is another of the many aspects of a board's responsibility.

Acting Collectively

One of the cardinal principles of effective participation is that individuals shall not speak for the board unless authorized to do so. Board action is a collective process which must be respected. Normally, the chair either exercises authority as spokesperson or appoints someone to perform in that capacity. Members may express views freely in meetings before voting, but after each vote, all involved are bound to abide by the decision. Any unauthorized expression in public could result in misinterpretation, promote disharmony, and affect board solidarity.

Considering the vagaries of human nature, a board may have difficulty keeping power focused on the group as an entity. Unfortunate it is when a single member, infatuated with visions of grandeur, arrogantly becomes self-appointed leader, thinker, and spokesperson. Equally detrimental is the political heavyweight or large donor who expects his or her membership and vote to carry special consideration. Effectively controlling such persons may test the mettle of the most skillful chairperson.

A board's important decisions are usually made in an atmosphere of uncertainty, speculation, and disagreement. Opportunities for dispute are manifold. To carry points of contention that arise into the public arena can be seriously dysfunctional, especially as one views the social and political overtones of many discussions. The lesson for new members is to act with decorum and in keeping with accepted mores.

When directing comments to administrators, members should be careful not to make statements which could be interpreted as expectations. Executives give credence to various comments, sometimes bestowing undue importance upon them. Even idle, off-the-cuff expressions of thought can emerge as perceived directives. Because an executive can serve only one master (the full board), all requests of administrators should be presented and discussed at a board meeting or be cleared first with the board's chairperson—and that practice should be made known and followed without exception.

Preparing Agenda

Agenda are programs of things to be done during meetings. Items for consideration are ordinarily recommended by the executive to the board's chairperson. By following accepted procedure, members of the board may also recommend items for discussion. A good set of bylaws will specify how.

Outsiders and employees should be allowed to have items placed on agenda only according to stated policy and only if, in the judgment of those in charge, the reasons are valid and pertinent to institutional purposes. It is extremely important for the executive to have full knowledge of any such request and the reason for it. Instances are on record where, for example, attempts have been made to promote topics different from those originally identified. A wise chairperson will not permit presentations of that sort, insisting, instead, that the true purpose be presented beforehand within administrative channels. To do otherwise is to weaken administrative authority and to invite repeated, unauthorized discussion. No administrator, no matter how competent, can be expected to forebear for long the consequences of being bypassed.

Agenda should have topics listed in a consistent order from one meeting to the next. A general order of business for a school or college may be as follows:

Call to Order
Review of Minutes
Financial Business
Institutional Development:
  Facilities
  Instruction/Curriculum
  Student Services
Personnel Matters
Executive's Report
Other Business
Adjournment

Not all items listed need be included each time. Only those which are relevant to the meeting should be included, and matters of development should be written in terms which are more specific than the topics shown.

Agenda must not be overloaded nor filled with unimportant topics. The executive officer can exercise judgment in this matter when planning meetings. Lengthy sessions are bound to happen at times, not only as a consequence of full agenda but also from failing to have the board prepared with background information leading to a recommendation on a complex issue. Except for an occasional unexpected crisis which defies planning, the board should be as thoroughly educated on new items as is reasonably possible. Having background information distributed with the agenda will often serve the purpose.

It is helpful, too, for some boards to receive carefully written resolutions on items requiring a vote. Some members seem to fear creating a motion. Others have difficulty stating a complete one. A written resolution can, at least in those situations, be beneficial from the standpoint of time and accuracy of record.

Insofar as possible, copies of agenda, supporting information, and minutes of each previous meeting should be mailed or delivered from the chief administrator's office to the members six or more days in advance of a scheduled meeting. Boards assembling less often than monthly, say quarterly, may benefit from still more lead time. The purpose is to be sure the members will have adequate time to prepare, yet not receive materials so far in advance that important, recent information cannot be included.

Conducting Meetings

Regularly scheduled meetings of a board of control are business meetings, and they should be conducted in a businesslike manner. Business meetings are not a place for social banter, small talk, or political discussions. They must be kept orderly, logical, and productive.

Members occasionally need reminding of the seriousness of their work. Institutional projects and developments usually have a life span longer than the tenure of the members present. An effective leader will not let this fact go unnoticed.

The person elected to the chair must maintain control of meetings. Firmness and courtesy in enforcing rules must be constantly maintained. Irrelevant rambling should be disallowed, the published order of topics should be rarely changed, and voting should occur in accordance with the bylaws. Permitting extraneous or unscheduled matters to be brought into meetings invites lengthy, unproductive, and even detrimental debate and discussion.

The meetings held by a certain private college board provide an uncommon, though pertinent, illustration of how a board can go astray. This unusual group met four times annually. Each meeting lasted two hours, no more and no less. Typically, the members began meetings by deliberating about which among them would be next in line to receive an honorary degree at their college's annual commencement. Their president's agenda on educational matters were considered only if time remained to do so. His concerns frequently went unattended. As could be expected, the board experienced difficulty retaining a president whose ego meshed with their own.

Meetings open to the public and press should be held to a program of scheduled activities, and those in charge must maintain control if confronted by a hostile group. Negative incidents can become disruptive unless the board's elected leader maintains tight control. Should that person fail to exercise appropriate authority, one would hope there are a few members present who have the courage to speak out for order. Anyone having no place in the program but attempting to be heard should be promptly informed of the restrictions. If an individual or group continues to interrupt or become demonstratively disruptive (as has been known to occur), one or all should be directed from the audience or, if necessary, the meeting adjourned. A board need not, and should not, tolerate actions disruptive of scheduled proceedings.

The person who elicits discussion from the audience during a business meeting likewise invites chaos. Some school board meetings are conducted that way. The problem is, perhaps more often than not, the press and many in attendance remember the complaints and criticisms better than anything else. The sound, constructive accomplishments being advanced seem often to be completely overshadowed.

When public testimony is desired, one way to proceed is to schedule an informal meeting apart from the business meeting. That practice seems to be the best of all the variations observed. It keeps the business meeting just what it is intended to be, while giving nonmembers a forum which cannot result in official action at that time. The comments need not be made part of a record or the official minutes.

Regular meetings proceed most orderly when the membership observes common courtesies. Waiting for a speaker to yield the floor before seeking recognition by the chair, discussing motions openly instead of whispering to neighbors, and addressing remarks to the group rather than toward one individual are among them. Simple courtesies can do much to avoid tension and hostility.

Also, the board should be reasonably well-versed in parliamentary procedures. The bylaws will ordinarily indicate which authority to reference. Although not a necessity for a smoothly functioning body, a member or the board's attorney can be designated *parliamentarian* for official meetings.

Keeping Minutes

The minutes of an official meeting are usually recorded by someone other than a board member. This is as it should be. All members must be totally free to think and to enter unhindered into discussions. Having a voting member both record minutes and exercise rights of debate and ballot increases the probability of one or neither activity being done adequately. Having the executive officer's secretary appointed as the board's recording secretary is the most logical practice from the standpoint of both executive and board.

The written record of a meeting should be brief, but it should describe all business transacted. Motions, who made and seconded them, and the vote occurring each time should be accurately recorded. Lengthy, verbatim discussions should not be included. At best, the minutes will show only if discussion occurred and a few high points. The recording secretary must never shade or distort what transpires, and any effort by that person to reflect a personal bias or to influence the outcome and intent of the board must not be condoned.

While a faithful record of fact remains the basic purpose, minutes sometimes reflect other intentions. They might be written for purposes of omitting embarrassing information, obscuring caveats or declarations for some readers, and for conditioning members about what to expect in the future. Some of these purposes are questionable; others serve a legitimate and useful function.

Boards representing publicly supported schools and colleges are generally required to keep minutes and to make them available upon reasonable request. The written record, like a meeting itself, is open to the public. Of importance in those situations is to be sure the minutes meet the requirements mandated by law. Executive sessions, that is, private sessions, should not be recorded, but any such session held during a regular meeting would be advisably noted in the minutes.

The notation should simply state the time and purpose along with verification of the session being called in accordance with the particular statute or regulation which applies.

Aside from legal requirements, there are other reasons for keeping minutes. An important one is the record provided and its value in future determinations. Another has to do with the expectations of accrediting agencies. For those reasons alone, private as well as public educational boards should take minutes regularly.

Observing the Sunshine Law

Sunshine laws are common. Many states have them. In general, the statutes require boards for tax-supported organizations to take official action and to conduct deliberations on business in meetings open to the public. They require giving notice to the public about the time, place, and purpose of any regular or special meeting. Another common requirement is to keep minutes in writing and available to the public for inspection.

Sunshine laws specify the conditions under which sessions may be excluded from public purview. Broadly stated, a closed session may be held for purposes of keeping certain sensitive matters confidential. Specifically permitted are discussions of personnel matters, security of facilities, the purchasing or selling of property, matters of impending or imminent court action, collective bargaining strategies, and other matters the disclosure of which would not be advantageous for the institution or the individuals involved. In any case, final action on a topic discussed behind closed doors must occur in an open meeting.

As a matter of essential practice, the law prevailing in the board's jurisdiction must be reviewed to be sure of its contents. The executive officer can keep the membership fully apprised. Legal counsel can be called upon to clarify meanings.

That boardrooms are no longer inaccessible is generally true, and the day has passed when members of public boards can meet entirely in private. All that seems to be a mixed blessing, however. Conducting virtually everything before the press and the constituents concerned, holding meetings to be legal only if previously announced (including gatherings or luncheon meetings of three or more members), and imposing penalties on members for any violation of the regulations are factors restrictive of the members while, at least potentially, working beneficially for others. In many instances the laws are probably unnecessary. Boards of education and trustees, bound as many are by a code of ethics and conflict-of-interest laws, seem to have achieved a record of operating positively without the extra restrictions.

Cases are known where sunshine laws have operated to the detriment of board functioning and participation. How one board reacted at the time the law came into effect in one state will illustrate. Three members promptly resigned because of the conditions imposed, and others expressed their belief the regulations would tend to stifle discussion. Some expressed fear of the possible complications and damage to their personal and business reputations resulting from publicly viewed debates over taxes, the awarding of contracts, and other delicate issues. Whether or not the loss of able participants has been restricted to this one incident cannot be said, but, undoubtedly, service on a public board has become less attractive than before the laws took effect.

Probably every board has a member who will not participate as effectively in open meetings as in closed ones. The member may be a very intelligent person who simply hesitates to raise a dissenting voice in a crowd of strangers. The result may be to avoid questioning the wisdom of proposals made in public, even to the point of allowing a motion of debatable merit to pass unchallenged. Repeated opportunities to exercise profound judgment may pass by. The sunshine law is at least partly counterproductive in that situation, and it is likely to remain so until an equally capable but more vocal replacement takes office.

The extent to which sunshine laws have operated in the public interest remains open to speculation. Some boards operating under the law have curtailed deliberating in secrecy, and some have been charged with discussing more topics behind closed doors than ever before. In general, boards have become more aware of the need to be above reproach in their practices concerning open disclosure. The propensity of people to sue has probably had something to do with this trend. At the same time, boards have become much more restrictive in their public statements and deliberations for fear of litigation. The experience seems inconclusive, though the law is well-intentioned.

Practicing Protocol and Ethics

The principles of protocol and ethics are extremely important. *Protocol* refers to the rules of etiquette and diplomacy to be observed within the group and in relations with the professional staff. *Ethics* consists of the rules of moral, or right, conduct. Neither term is strictly legalistic in intent, although they may be reinforced with official backing.

In practice, individual participants should be sufficiently educated in matters of etiquette to apply them when interfacing with others. Moreover, they are expected to follow the chain of command. Just as employees are encouraged to observe the institution's hierarchy of control, board members should always work with their chairperson and the chief executive when planning to meet with subordinate employees. This expectation is more than mere courtesy. It is recognition and reinforcement of the organizational structure on which order, authority, and control reside.

Practicing the rules of ethics and protocol does not mean that everyone must always agree, either within the controlling body or with administrators. Always doing so could be tantamount to abdicating responsibility. Frequent rebuffs are another matter. Repeated criticism and disparagement of a colleague's ideas creates tension and could lead to hostility. The administrative officer who suffers frequent defeats or open criticism at the hands of the board will probably soon lose a measure of prestige, authority, and loyal support among staff and faculty.

Ethical conduct among members of controlling boards means they must observe the oath of office, abstain from deliberating and voting on matters of potential conflict of interest, make no behind-the-scenes attempt to influence a vote for personal benefit or some special interest, and file, if required by law, proper financial disclosure statements. Once again prevailing statutes should be made available, but with or without any legal reference, the board would be well-advised to develop a code of ethics. This practice would be advisable in almost any situation, for the principles of ethics appropriate for conducting business are far more extensive than as ordinarily written into law. Comprehensive statements of ethics are the hallmark of a conscientious board.

Using Committees

Committees should be used judiciously. Some wisdom may be noted in an analysis of the oft-quoted line, "While Nero fiddled, Rome burned." Pundits have sometimes questioned whether Nero was engaged in a committee meeting, surrounded by councils of wise men who were engrossed in planning the city's future.

Committees appointed from a board's membership can serve a

useful purpose, of course. They are especially beneficial when (1) the institution is growing and much work remains to be accomplished on many fronts, (2) board and staff are confronted with an extraordinary amount of work on a special problem or unique task, and (3) the board as a whole meets on an infrequent basis. In committee, a few members and their executive can devote more time to a topic than can comfortably occur with the full contingency in regular session, and the expertise attained through extensive participation by a few will often be accepted as evidence the committee's recommendations are worthy of adopting. The combined thrust of several committees supporting executive recommendations on different issues can be very positive. Furthermore, committee work is often accomplished in an atmosphere of complete freedom for discussion. Constituents and the press seldom show interest in attending meetings of committees deliberating over educational concerns.

On the other hand, committees are not entirely necessary when conditions are relatively stable, the board is small, and the full membership meets regularly on a monthly basis or more often. Their use may actually be contrary to good board functioning under those conditions. Committee work excludes a portion of the membership from fundamental considerations, with participation and understanding by the full board being sacrificed to a significant extent. The most serious loss is likely where a committee has been delegated authority to act without review of its decisions by the entire body of control.

One of the main problems with board committees is their tendency to become involved in administrative detail. For that reason, committee structure and functioning should be periodically evaluated. Executives, if asked, will usually be completely candid in identifying areas of encroachment on administrative prerogative. Boards must learn to restrict their involvement to policy making and planning.

Two or three standing committees are probably enough for carrying out special assignments. One dealing with finances and, perhaps, fund raising, another with personnel, salaries, and negotiations; and possibly a third with some phase of institutional development, such as land acquisition or board in-service training, should suffice. Discussions on long-range planning should not be delegated to a committee. Without exception, that is an area warranting total board involvement and decision making.

Developing Job Descriptions

Every board needs complete descriptions of duties for its members, officers, and standing committees. The descriptions serve as a valuable operational guide. They are especially useful to new members and to newly elected officers in their efforts to adjust.

While published lists of duties are available, each body would benefit by developing its own. The process of creating the descriptions can be helpful in itself. It achieves the maximum in involvement, commitment, and compliance.

Next to a set of bylaws and policies, written job descriptions are a most useful tool. Properly written descriptions help avoid encroachment on administrative responsibilities by defining specific areas of accountability, and they serve as the basis for the board's evaluation. As with bylaws and policies, the statements must undergo periodic review. All members can profit thereby.

The chief administrator can provide leadership in the process. Initially he may have to motivate a lethargic board to action, but after the idea gains acceptance, he can supply sample descriptions from which comparisons and development can proceed. His involvement in later evaluations may also be needed.

Weak boards seem to resist or somehow avoid the use of job descriptions. Strong boards welcome them, and the fact that they do indicates a manner of operating from which their strength derives.

Bargaining with Faculty

The advent of and trend toward organized collective bargaining in educational institutions throughout the states have brought on a plethora of publications and expert advice. Manuals and consultants in large numbers exist in the marketplace. In view of the available assistance and the critical, often unique nature of the process, only a few precautionary words of advice about collective bargaining will be given here.

Some unfortunate mistakes have been made in the early stages of bargaining with faculty that can be avoided. Here are several directives worthy of observing that have emerged over the years: First, seek expert advice from a point prior to union election and into contract negotiation, and employ a successful negotiator to work with the administrative team and represent the institution. Second, have the board remain in the background, limiting its role to major decisions, encouragement of the management team, and ratification of the contract. Third, follow a policy which prohibits individuals on the board from becoming a conduit for a voice weakening the negotiation team's position. Fourth, and last to be mentioned here, establish a policy of close board-executive cooperation, including the mutual development of agreements on management rights, the need for protecting and maintaining authority, and assurance of quality in the programs and services for students. Although intended for union shops, at least several of these recommendations are apropos in places pursuing informal negotiations.

For authorities uninitiated in the tactics of faculty unions, a word of warning is offered: Be prepared to be discredited in the local press. Management-union negotiation is an adversarial process. It is common for faculty to attempt to split board-executive solidarity and publicly call for resignations. Discrediting those who do not support the faculty's demands is an old, vicious, and occasionally effective tactic. Neither capitulation or appeasement is the answer. Emanual Kant's philosophy is an appropriate guide in those situations. "The greatest good," Kant said, "is to do one's duty apart from inclination."

Improving Board Performance

The effectiveness of a controlling body depends to a noteworthy extent on individual members observing the laws, rules, codes, and customs which prevail. A high level of effectiveness can be attained only if all recognize the limitations of service, understand the needs of employees, remain sensitive to the needs of students, preserve the institution and its purpose, and keep a broad view at all times. Improvement in performance on a board may be as contingent upon the members' potential at the time of selection as are subsequent efforts toward their edification.

An able board will sense change and analyze trends when planning. Some boards deal too much with past and present problems instead of looking ahead in an effort to develop offsetting strategies. Over-attention to the past gives rise to the rehashing of problems, concerns, and weaknesses, while providing a forum for those who feel mistreated. The present is but a passing moment and cannot command much attention, or it, too, will lead a board down the path of excessive retrospection. Properly oriented, a board will direct considerable attention to the short- and long-range planning needed for achieving and preserving institutional quality and ideals.

As a basis for planning, a progressive board will persistently raise questions about the institution's standards, achievements, and ideas for improving learning. Queries of that nature are especially important in this era of seemingly mediocre output. In the final analysis, the board's part in achieving progress is its measure of effectiveness. An appropriately written set of job descriptions will virtually compel the members to think in terms of results.

Chapter 4

Defining Goals and Setting Policy

All planning is for the future. Tomorrow's progress is inextricably related to the quality of the planning occurring today. In education, boards and executives share responsibility for looking ahead. If a board superficially addresses its institution's future, planning will be left almost entirely to the discretion of the chief administrator and any team of assistants he or she might assemble. If, on the other hand, the board attempts to establish goals and policy without meaningful input by knowledgeable educators, it risks failure not only from making uninformed decisions but also from not involving professionals whose support is needed to implement any worthy decision that might be forthcoming. The future of a school or college is best charted through cooperative development of goals and policies as they relate to the institution's mission.

Reviewing Mission and Philosophy

The board of control represents the pinnacle in the hierarchy of authority in educational organizations, with its authority deriving mainly from the state's statutes or a charter. Its legal status and vested powers are founded on assurances the school or college will operate in conformity with laws of the state in which it is located. Whether the institution is profit making or nonprofit does not affect a board's authority or liability significantly. Its mission as a church-related, independent, or public organization does make a difference on the board's operation, of course.

Mission and philosophy are inherently related. *Mission* is the special service to be performed, the purpose. *Philosophy* is the system of beliefs and principles which direct action toward the mission's implementation and achievement. In practice, philosophy is an expression of the value system of persons establishing the institution's mission and of those working to fulfill it.

The board which asks, as one frequently should, "Why are we here?" or "What is this institution to do?" is seeking clarification or reaffirmation of purposes. Questions of that nature are the beginning point for planning. While the inquiries may reaffirm a purpose of providing effectively for learning, they must also lead to recognition of the special direction the mission denotes. Adult vocational school, liberal arts college, comprehensive community college, and parochial elementary school are identifiers for institutions having different missions.

A controlling body's philosophical bent can lead to other differences, even among organizations of the same type and mission. For example, one vocational school might provide a narrowly structured, intensive course of specialized training at a single level, while another might build its program more comprehensively by incorporating a liberal portion of general studies, career guidance, continuing education, and social and civic development within a complex of occupational studies and choices. Such differences are most apparent in comparisons of company-operated and publicly-funded vocational schools.

Theoretically, a board may do whatever is necessary for achieving an authorized mission. In actuality, a board is limited by federal, state, and local laws and regulations, by the institution's charter, by its own rules and policies, and by the degree to which its actions are accepted by different constituencies. Any of these factors can affect decisions about an institution's future.

From time to time, a board should review the statements of mission and philosophy it follows as a basis for strategically planning and setting goals for the years ahead. An orderly review helps when establishing the parameters for change. Furthermore, new interpretations may be needed to keep abreast cultural demands and the dynamics of a progressive civilization. History makes this clear. The need to keep guiding values current is evident through reflecting on the now outmoded Swedish Sloyd System of manual arts once taught in secondary schools. Similarly outdated is the once common emphasis by our founding universities to prepare students mainly for the clergy, government, and a few professions. Our current systems of delivery could also become fettered by diminishing needs, unless those in authority continually address the issue with critical questions.

Developing Goals

Goals are milestones derived from statements of mission and philosophy. They provide measures across time against which progress can be assessed. Although often neglected, goal setting and assessment represent the epitome of board service.

As with philosophy, a board should rely heavily on educators when establishing goals for the institution. Administrators can suggest targets for the institution's long-term development, possibly for five-year and ten-year periods. These should be updated annually when setting short-term goals for the year ahead. Once adopted by the board, the statements provide direction for developments in the areas identified.

Goals also provide a means of holding personnel accountable for improvements. The chief executive, working with administrative subordinates, can have the goals internalized into specific, supplementary objectives within each organizational unit. Of importance in this respect is to compare the results achieved to the stated targets. This might be done annually, sharing the data with the board in preparation for updating current goals or adopting new ones.

For purposes of discussion, a distinction may be made between goals and objectives. Goals are ordinarily written in general terms. Objectives, when associated with goal statements, are stated more specifically and, preferably, in measurable terms.

An example may help clarify the difference. A goal written as it might be set by a board could be as broad in scope as this: *Improvement in the finances of (school or college)*. An objective related to this goal should show what is to be done, when it is to be done, the level of improvement expected, and who is responsible. Only by making those matters clear can the results be measured against some standard and can somebody be held accountable. Here is an objective that satisfies these criteria: *The Community Services Department shall obtain a 10 percent increase in philanthropic support during the next year*. Other objectives for the same goal could specify a reduction of expenditures in certain academic units, installing a security device in the library to reduce losses, and taking steps to put extra curricular activities on a profitable basis. The possibilities are extensive. Their final form will depend not only on interpretations of mission and philosophy, but also on conditions existing in each situation.

An awareness and acceptance of the goals adopted by the board is enhanced by working with the persons responsible for their achievement, but little is gained by developing goals cooperatively and then allowing them to be ignored. Their inclusion in a master plan document will emphasize their importance. A practice of holding individuals accountable for results in each area will improve the institution's overall performance.

Writing the Master Plan

The responsibility for developing a master plan, sometimes referred to as a school or college's *long-range plan,* should be assigned to the executive officer and his staff. The board holds authority for review and approval. While the writing and compiling of information could involve many employees, final approval of the plan properly occurs by the board of control on the recommendation of the executive officer. Statements of philosophy, goals, and objectives particularly warrant close analysis at the top levels of governance.

Basically, a master plan is a document explaining where the unit or system has been, where it is now, and where it is going. It is a guide for faculty, staff, and board for the entity's direction over a period of some five years. Longer periods invariably invite less definitive planning. In any case, the importance of including relatively precise standards for the first years of the plan should not be overlooked.

The content of such a document may be as follows:

I.   Institutional Background and Setting
II.   Characteristics of the Service Area
III.   Characteristics of the Institution
IV.   Foundation Plan (Mission, Philosophy, and Goals)
V.   Plan for Academic Services
VI.   Plan for Student Services
VII.   Plan for Business Services
VIII. Plan for Administration and Governance
IX.   Summary of Future Developments

Background information, demographic data, and district (or service area) characteristics are fundamental to the logical development of standards and projections for the future. An analysis of conditions pertaining to students, finances, facilities, personnel, programs, and services constitutes a basic approach to master planning. Identification of the strengths and weaknesses of various internal components is an equally important part of the process, because projections cannot be made confidently without the depth of knowledge such analyses produce. When completed, the plan's usefulness will correlate with the quality of the effort that went into its preparation.

Arriving at this point in planning may not always be easy. Some boards do not even see the need to put policies in writing, let alone broad guidelines for the future. Nevertheless, an experienced educator will insist that a comprehensively planned document be made available. Master planning can be among the most important activities in which a governing board will become involved, as the experience of working with professionals in the development of a scholarly plan can be very positive. Constituent groups will have evidence of institutional planning being taken seriously, but, more important, employees will have a thorough guide by which to mold and direct their activities.

Setting Policy and Bylaws

Whereas a written master plan is extremely useful, a policy manual is virtually essential. Conscientious boards make use of both types of documents. Yet, one may occasionally hear that a particular operation has continued for as long as twenty years without having policies put into writing. How a people-centered organization can maintain the stability, coordination of duties, and orderly direction of operations desired without the certainty of written rules and regulations is truly amazing. Such a practice, to say the least, represents unbusinesslike procedure. Repetition, inconsistency, and contradiction in decision making are the probable results. In addition to inviting disorganization, ever-increasing opportunities abound for legal action and loss of accreditation or federal funding. Affirmative action in hiring and promotion, to choose a topic of legal import, is one area in which a published policy statement can be of utmost importance. A statement prohibiting sexual harassment in the workplace is another example. It, too, represents an area for which a statement of policy can regulate behavior while setting out the board's action for noncompliance.

One of the first needs is a statement of the requirements to be met for adopting polices. This statement should make allowance for constituent input and sufficient time for reviewing each statement before its adoption. Serious confrontational behavior might be avoided by consulting with those directly affected. The following four elements of control might also be helpful if covered in the statement:

1.   Affirmation of purpose and authority of the board in policy making.

2.   Procedure for adopting policy statements, such as only at regular meetings and after two readings.

3.   Power of the executive in making recommendations and rules relative to policy, or to act in its absence.

4.   Procedure for reviewing and changing policy statements.

The final precautionary suggestion presented here is to put into policy only that which is expected to be followed. Policy, for purposes of organizational control, must be followed to the letter. The board should make this expectation clear. If a policy is bad or inadequate, it should be revised or eliminated. Violations should not be tolerated. Otherwise, employees may act as they see fit.

This same expectation should apply to the board. The body which acts contrary to its own policy (and there have been such) will surely inspire a loss of confidence among staff and faculty. Holding anyone accountable for failure to follow the rules and regulations would likely be difficult when the board itself violates the provisions. Congruence between institutional policy and the actions of employees is essential for effective functioning.

Compiling the Manual

School and college policies should be typed and arranged for distribution in notebook form. The bylaws, the procedural rules by which the board operates, are placed near the beginning. Ordinarily included are topics defining the board's powers, membership, officers, regular and special meetings, quorum, committees, rules for adopting policy, and procedures for amending policies. Regulations on nondiscrimination, conflict of interest, and affirmative action, in addition to statements on compensation, duties of members and officers, and powers of the executive might also be placed in this section of the manual.

The bulk of the manual is devoted to the policies applicable to personnel and functional divisions within the college, school, or system. Any logical method of grouping that simplifies referencing is acceptable. Besides the board's policies, the statements might be assembled according to (1) the purposes and guiding philosophy of the organization, (2) the organizational structure, (3) policies affecting students, from admission through graduation, (4) personnel matters, including employment standards, working conditions, duties, cause for dismissal, and academic freedom, (5) the educational program, (6) auxiliary enterprises, (7) use and maintenance of the physical plant and equipment, and (8) financial regulations and procedures.

The contents of the part dealing with curricular matters will vary according to specific circumstances. The educational program necessarily occupies an essential place in the policy-making role of boards where the state's minimums for elementary and secondary schools must be satisfied. There, the policies are likely to be highly detailed. In colleges and universities, as a rule, the policy manual will contain only general statements about curricular matters, thereby allowing faculty and staff much discretion and freedom in making decisions about the educational program. The institution's catalog provides details and receives the board's official backing by resolution, usually about the time of publication.

Following is an outline for a slightly different arrangement of a policy manual:

A. General
B. Board of Control
C. Administrative Personnel and Functions
D. Faculty and Related Professionals
E. Classified Personnel
F. Student Services
G. Academic Services
H. Business Services
I. Auxiliary Services
J. Appendix

In this system, the first section is devoted to the broadly applicable topics of purposes, organization, and certain matters of employment, such as rights of due process, nondiscrimination, and grievance procedures. The section on administration clarifies exactly which positions are supervisory—a matter of considerable importance for excluding positions from the collective bargaining unit where such exists. It, as with other sections about personnel, can be supplemented with descriptions of applicable positions and job duties. A table of contents, an introductory statement, and an appendix which contains copies of relevant laws will enhance the usefulness of the document.

When preparing a manual, administrators will ordinarily consult sets of policies followed elsewhere. The board or its committee might ask to review such documents when planning to adopt one or more statements. While differences in wording are likely, the topics are very similar from one manual to the next. The lists of topics in Fig. 4.1 for sections B and C of the previous outline shows what can be expected.

<table>
<tr><td>B. Board of Control</td><td>C. Administrative Personnel</td></tr>
<tr><td>1. Membership</td><td>1. Classifications</td></tr>
<tr><td>2. Election/Appointment</td><td>2. Supervisory Controls</td></tr>
<tr><td>3. Duties of Members</td><td>3. Chief Executive</td></tr>
<tr><td>4. Powers and Authority</td><td>4. Officers</td></tr>
<tr><td>5. Compensation</td><td>5. Duties</td></tr>
<tr><td>10. Organization</td><td>10. Selection/Appointment</td></tr>
<tr><td>11. Officers and Duties</td><td>11. Contract Renewal</td></tr>
<tr><td>12. Committees</td><td>12. Medical Examination</td></tr>
<tr><td>13. Attorney</td><td>13. Payroll</td></tr>
<tr><td>15. Meetings</td><td>15. Medical Leave</td></tr>
<tr><td>16. Quorum</td><td>16. Maternity Leave</td></tr>
<tr><td>17. Minutes</td><td>17. Sabbatical Leave</td></tr>
<tr><td>18. Agenda</td><td>18. Special Leave</td></tr>
<tr><td>19. Parliamentary Procedure</td><td>19. Insurance</td></tr>
<tr><td>20. Policy Adoption, Review, Revision Procedures</td><td>20. Vacations</td></tr>
<tr><td>25. Code of Ethics</td><td>25. Outside Commitments</td></tr>
<tr><td></td><td>26. Tutoring/Related Act.</td></tr>
<tr><td></td><td>27. Professional Development Plan</td></tr>
</table>

Figure 4.1 Topical Divisions for a Policy Manual

Notice the use of numbering so that policy statements can be entered later where desired. Whatever system is adopted, it should be followed consistently throughout.

Statements for each topic should be brief and to the point. Any ambiguous or unclear statement should be revised at the earliest opportunity.

As policy making is not a static process, the manual should be constructed for ease in revision. The use of a loose-leaf binder is recommended. Another suggestion is to place only one policy, or no more than two short policies, on a single page. A record kept by a responsible secretary of the manuals in circulation will facilitate the updating chore.

The decision to include or not to include rules with policy statements is discretional. The two are different. A *policy* is a guideline which the board adopts officially to direct a course of action or make a statement of fact. A *rule* gives the detailed procedure for putting a policy into practice. Generally, rules are developed by administrators, but on occasion, a board will act on procedures for implementing a policy. It is appropriate to include in the manual any regulation the board has adopted, be it policy or rule. Administrator's rules should be kept in a separate reference. In each case, dates of adoption and revision should be included as applicable.

Fulfilling the Task

The board member who begins to realize the weight of responsibility in planning, the care with which goals and policies must be set, and the attention to philosophy and mission necessary for effective participation shows signs of alertness to the demands of the office. Board service produces no casual course for a conscientious person. Only those failing to view their obligation seriously find there is little work to do.

For the new member, the reading and understanding of documents described in this chapter can be a formidable task by itself. A policy manual and master plan will usually be available upon assuming a place on the board. In the absence of such, the need should be made known. An early understanding of the institution's mission, philosophy, goals, and policies as established is important for carrying out responsibilities and developing any guidelines which follow.

Chapter 5

Budgeting and Building

Finance and facilities are among the main concern of authorities in education. There are two important reasons why. First, responsible persons want to create a positive history during their tenure by leaving a legacy of having built or maintained a sound operation. Second, they will most likely be remembered favorably for accomplishments that are tangible and personally identifiable. A building remains as visible evidence for a long time, and a plaque placed near its entrance assigns primary credit. On the other hand, prolonged financial crises and demands for huge increases in tuition or tax revenues can have the opposite effect. Both fiscal soundness and adequacy of the physical plant are minimum expectations. They are essential conditions for learning to flourish.

Effective board service requires the membership of people who have at least a rudimentary knowledge of financial matters and plant development and maintenance. The responsibility cannot be avoided. Whether or not prepared to do so, boards must make numerous decisions about revenues, fund raising, budgeting, purchasing, salaries and, in times of scarcity of resources, downsizing. As to facilities, they might be faced with choices about building design, construction, renovation, contracting, repairs, site drainage, utilities, vehicle storage, educational equipment, furnishings, and so forth. The magnitude of these concerns becomes further apparent when viewed in a dollars-and-cents comparison. The total of an institution's operating budget and investment in the plant may exceed the combined personal assets of the board many times over. Personal experience limited to mortgaging one's home and keeping a family budget represent only a meager beginning in that environment.

In all likelihood, few members of a board will have acquired in-depth experience in each area of responsibility. This chapter can neither change that nor make experts of novices. Its purpose is to provide suggestions for gaining a working knowledge of the two processes.

Budgeting and Financing

Just as one need not live in a nuclear reactor in order to understand nuclear engineering, a person need not be a bookkeeper or an accountant to be a board member. Specialists are available in the business office, and others may be employed as consultants if needed. The average member's role is to learn enough about fiscal procedures to make reasonably good judgments without relying completely on the knowledge of a specialist, including instances when an accountant is a member of the board.

The professional role of the specialist who occupies a place on the board deserves understanding and protecting. Although expertise should never be ignored, no board member no matter how informed should be asked to do the extensive work ordinarily required in day-to-day activities. Care must be taken not to make demands which exceed the limits of ethicality.

An accountant-member might be particularly helpful, nevertheless. An example is serving on a committee to select an accounting firm for the annual audit or to review the findings when the audit team has been appointed by the state. The specialist's input can be invaluable in such instances, as long as all semblance of conflict of interest is avoided.

Board members generally understand what a budget is, and they devote much attention to seeing that their's remains balanced. A meeting seldom passes without some budgetary detail being routinely or placidly discussed, but an unbalanced fiscal projection placed before the board will begin to draw expressions of anxiety. In cases of severe shortfall, the mood could change to outright alarm and despair. The difficulties foreshadowed by an unbalanced budget can make board service an utterly trying experience.

Living within One's Means

Of the reasons institutions encounter financial difficulty, there is only one condition which cannot be legitimately overcome. That one is the absolute unavailability of financial resources. Such conditions seldom exist. More often, the finances do not provide for all things at the levels desired.

The management of scarcity can be more difficult for some than others. Sufficient revenue to offset inflation is a common problem, but add to this poor management of the resources already available and the difficulties grow. Some people become so comfortable operating in good times that they seem unable to curtail their habits when needed, continuing without restraint to feed a "caviar" appetite on a "potato" income.

The first requisite of institutional leadership is fiscal responsibility. Proficiency in planning, allocating resources, and holding personnel accountable is essential. Unless available dollars are being spent as effectively as reasonably possible, there can be no excuse for again tapping the taxpayer or hiking tuition, as school and college boards often do to increase revenue.

Many educators, supported by unknowing boards, are guilty of traditional incrementalism. Commonly, they develop the annual budget with expenses listed at a percentage greater than the year before. Any "fat" from previous years is carried over and enlarged as a legitimate expense. The increments seem to relate to priorities only superficially. Deficit budgets, financial crises, and urgent appeals for more revenue are among the possibilities.

Planning before Budgeting

Instead of preparing each budget incrementally, annual projections of operating costs should be based on objectives and the costs of programs and services needed to attain those objectives. To do that, the executive and fiscal officers must relate the budget to plans for the year ahead. Wasteful practices and ineffective programs can then be eliminated before money is allocated for their continuation. The achievement of institutional goals becomes the main thrust.

The board has an obligation to disallow poor budgeting under all circumstances. Although board members do not prepare the budget, they must be assured the one recommended for their adoption has been logically developed. There can be no room for laxity in this regard. Even if current resources are ample, expectations of competency and frugality in budgeting should be made clear. As protector of institutional interests, a board cannot tolerate administrative responses to probing questions about the budgeting process that indicate a lack of thoroughness in planning or little effort to keep expenditures in check.

Planning should begin early. Ordinarily, six months or more lead time is desired. By having defined institutional goals sufficiently ahead of the fiscal year, enough time will remain for setting objectives, activities, program plans, and priorities within the different departments. Such planning should always precede the allocation of funds. The process described in Chapter 4 is the starting point.

Involving Personnel

A budget is an estimate of revenues and expenditures for a specified period that can be relied on only to the extent the needs are accurately defined. This suggests the knowledge existing within the departments should be utilized, for specialists at the operational level are best positioned for identifying the processes and resources for their activities. Further, no better way can be devised for gaining support than by involving in the planning those directly responsible for the educational activities. Grassroots involvement can be extremely important for understanding when tradeoffs among cost and activities become necessary.

Budget requests often exceed resource limits, especially on the first go round. For that reason, each department's requests should be ranked within the limits set forth. Initial reductions, increases, and eliminations can then occur at this level. As effective decisions must be made at this stage of planning and resource allocation, executive leadership and coordination by the budget officer becomes essential.

The board exercises control in the planning process by approving institutional goals and, on occasion, establishing major parameters within which funds shall be spent. The board's usual practice is simply to charge the administration with relating expenditures to goals while keeping costs within estimated revenues. At other times, distributions among contingencies and the major operating accounts are suggested. The board becomes most actively involved thereafter when reviewing and acting upon the planned distributions.

Putting It Together

The balancing of expenditures and income can be nightmarish. Operational expenses constitute about twenty percent of the total budget. This provides for such things as supplies, travel, printing, mailing, equipment, upkeep, and utilities. A five-percent contingency allocation might be included if permissible and conditions are favorable for doing it. The remainder is for "big ticket" items: employee's salaries, wages, and benefit costs. Since many operational expenses are fixed or vary because of inflation, the opportunities for reducing non-payroll costs are limited.

Budgeting can seldom be done in a straightforward manner. It usually involves much back-and-forth input until reworked versions of income and expenses can be balanced out. With compensation of employees holding such a prominent place, can there be flexibility in budgeting? One thing boards (and administrators) must do is learn to reward employees on the basis of performance. If, for instance, improved learning is a goal, hard evidence of such improvement should be forthcoming before increasing pay for faculty beyond a cost of living adjustment. Simply laying out money in the hope of gaining friendship without holding personnel to meaningful standards of performance demonstrates serious disregard for measures of accountability.

Ideally, the first thing is to provide for necessities. Pay increases and new positions can then be approved on the residual. Employees, whether unionized or not, often negotiate for all the board will give them and without regard for other factors. Increases in revenue through tuition hikes or higher taxes seem to be too often the response to the demands. Fiscal restraint may be the proper answer. The wise board will keep this and institutional purposes in mind, and it will allocate the resources within the confines of a balanced budget.

Wherever permitted by law, the board should insist on budgeting for contingency expenses. Contingencies may be anticipated or unanticipated. The former include, by way of illustration, building repairs which can be expected to occur in time, although their exact cost and time of occurrence cannot be precisely predicted. The latter are needs which have been overlooked or simply develop as a consequence of unpredictable circumstances. An unusual act of vandalism and excessive unemployment claims are examples of this type.

Income and costs for the building and renovating of facilities are not ordinarily included in an operating budget. Except for routine maintenance, the revenue is frequently earmarked for a specific purpose. That being the case a major project is often budgeted separately.

Building and Maintaining Facilities

Considerations about building and maintaining school and college facilities, topics to be covered in the remainder of this chapter, can become very complex. How complex depends on circumstances. Certainly, the planning of a new building or an entire campus entails far more decision making than does the conversion of a heating plant from one fuel to another, but such decisions at almost all levels will require the input of persons having specialized knowledge. The board makes final decisions based on what it believes to be the best advice.

The board's decision-making responsibilities can be eased somewhat by an informed executive. Any executive, with the assistance of staff, must be able to keep the plant in repair and functioning. That person must also know when to refer problems to the board, including when to recommend employing an outside consultant.

A well-informed administrator or consultant with experience in education can perform a host of valuable functions, such as preparing preventive maintenance and energy saving plans, giving advice on alternate solutions to projects, planning and updating a facilities master plan, and writing educational specifications for equipment purchases. The services will supplement those of an architect or engineer employed for a particular project. Their use can lead to hugh savings. However helpful this may be, the board must still make major decisions on various aspects of a building and maintenance program. A special committee of the board might be helpful in these matters.

A board's involvement can be very extensive. Considerations relative to educational programming, site selection or building location, whether to build or renovate, sharing facilities, and selecting materials and furnishings are representative areas of concern. The problem is to keep focused on the major aspects of a building and maintenance program.

The danger of becoming too engrossed in the details of purchasing supplies and materials can easily befall a board. These are matters which generally should be deferred to administrators and any specialist employed at the time. Interesting tales of overinvolvement by boards are common among educators, and any administrator who has experienced much building probably has heard several of such stories. Some are humorous and some are downright pathetic.

In one known case, a board spent several hours, passing around samples of toilet paper, stacking one roll upon another, while comparing weights, textures, and prices. The members argued long and loud before making a selection for the school. During the final minutes of the meeting, they voted without discussion to purchase a piece of equipment which carried a price tag far in excess of the cost of a supply of the toilet article for about two years.

Another board, this one overseeing a construction project, met daily for a full week to choose brick for their school's new building. One meeting actually extended into the wee morning hours. Frequent motions to end the debate by making a decision at a specified time went unheeded. A decision was finally made after the architect hired a bricklayer to build samples walls, mortar and all, in the preferred colors. What was the decision? Interestingly, the brick selected was the one recommend by the architect in the first place. About the only thing accomplished by this exercise was heightened tension and extended animosity among certain members.

While paper-stacking and bricklaying episodes may happen more often than we realize, knowledgeable boards are less inclined to become engrossed in detail. They realize the advantage of relying on the judgment of professionals, and they know that doing so does not in many instances represent a loss of authority.

Developing a Facilities Plan

An up-to-date comprehensive plan for building and maintaining an institution's facilities affords a functional set of guidelines for orderly decision making. The plan directs the board's attention to needs of major importance, with opportunities for systematically reviewing progress in such areas as equipment maintenance, repair, and replacement. Data are presented of use in deciding the types, priorities, and timing of projects, as well as the resource requirements. School and college campuses on which the buildings appear uncoordinated in style and construction are examples of what can happen without having a long-range plan for facilities development in place.

The facilities plan is an adjunct to the institution's educational master plan, defining essentially how the school or college's physical plant meets or does not meet current needs and what must be done to accommodate students and offerings in the years ahead. Both institutional goals and enrollment projections form the basis of a plan. Projected courses and services, in turn, help define the needs ahead for facilities and capital funding. Whether the facilities plan becomes part of an institutional master plan or is set apart in another document is not the important concern. Reasonable accuracy in projecting is important.

Who should prepare the document? Here, again, a cooperative effort works best. Staff, faculty, and board should all take part, with someone on the staff assigned to coordinate the effort.

The facilities plan will be most useful if comprehensive. Some recommended topics, or sections, are: (a) Building and Grounds (description and value as existing), (b) Equipment and Furnishings (description, cost, and condition), (c) The Maintenance Program (personnel, maintenance schedules, problem areas), (d) Projected Academic Programs and Student Services (additions, and changes), (e) Projected Facilities Needs (equipment, furnishings, vehicles, and building spaces over the next five years), (f) The Facilities Development Program (schedule for buildings and equipment replacement, renovation, and new), and (g) Appendix (supplemental data, e.g., state standards and utilization data).

Much might be stated in the plan that the foregoing outline does not show. The more cost data and comparative analyses included, generally, the more information likely to be available for making intelligent decisions. Examples of such are: utility costs per pupil and per cubic foot for each building, calculated by year; weekly room utilization rates; assignable square footage per building, classroom, and laboratory; space and station occupancy rates; efficiency, such as ratios of operating costs to utilization; and comparisons of maintenance costs and building values. The purpose of such computations is not merely to describe assets numerically but to present facts and probabilities so the most effective uses of resources can be determined.

The various values obtained may be compared with data available from private and public sources. State education departments and regents' offices often accumulate data from within their state. The accumulated data, usually released in aggregate form, serve as excellent guiding standards, or averages, in addition to indicating which types of calculations to make for a systematic comparison.

Just as an administration's inability to provide adequate comparative data for consideration cannot be excused, there can be no justification for the board turning to students and taxpayers for additional operating and capital funds when it has not made certain the dollars available for the physical plant are being used economically and effectively. Undoubtedly, some boards and administrators are remiss for not being more cost conscious. They seemingly too often pursue carefully orchestrated propaganda campaigns in place of hard-and-fast evidence of need. Those asked to foot the bill will often capitulate without ever knowing the relevant facts.

Building and Renovating

A good plan will indicate when to refurbish a building or when to add one. New educational programs and services for students, structurally or functionally unsafe quarters, or an increasing student population are several customary identifiers of need for new facilities. Even where adequate plant space exists, the evidence will show that continual repair and renovation do not always produce the best of alternatives. Ordinarily, however, some renovation and re-allocation of space will accompany new building construction.

The board, once made aware of the probable need for new construction or major renovation, should request a thorough study of need and feasibility. The study is a refinement of a part of the more broadly conceived facilities plan. It should precede the employment of a firm for designing the project, although a professional might assist on a preliminary consulting basis.

The results of the study should show, convincingly if possible, the reasons for selecting a particular course of action. Comparisons of initial costs are not enough. Operating costs over the life of the alternates, their relative safety, construction advantages, functional qualities, available funds, etcetera, are also needed, and the conclusions should be made known. Doing so may enhance the board's reputation for credibility and sound decision making. It may even avoid the embarrassment of facing an obstreperously skeptical group or a vexatious press.

The decision to build or to renovate entails a variety of subsequent steps. Those of principal concern to the board include the following:

1. Employing an architect or engineer
2. Obtaining the funds
3. Approving educational specifications
4. Approving design and working drawings
5. Letting bids and employing a construction firm
6. Breaking ground, reviewing progress, and approving change orders
7. Accepting the completed project

Considerably more is involved than this list suggests. Unforeseen problems also arise at times. One such might be a labor strike over union-shop matters. An attentive board will be aware of the legal requirements in this and other areas of the process.

Employing an Architect

The employment of an architect or architectural firm when planning to renovate or construct facilities can involve more than first meets the eye. The responsibility can easily be underestimated. The initial impact of a building project and its effectiveness throughout years of use are largely a consequence of who has been selected to do the design work.

Before signing an agreement, the board should establish a selection procedure. Design competition and closed bidding procedures are permissible but seldom used except in extraordinarily large projects. The direct selection process is preferred in education. When done thoroughly, the procedure is as follows:

1. Set major guidelines for the project
2. Establish selection criteria and qualifications
3. Identify qualified individuals or firms
4. Inform candidates and request applications
5. Select the top candidates
6. Interview several candidates
7. Visit representative projects
8. Choose the best candidate
9. Negotiate the contract

Regardless of the previous experience among the board, the members should collectively review what needs to be done and together decide how to progress from step to step. Each project is unique, and each demands the combined thought and deliberation of the entire membership.

As a final thought on this topic, each board should decide what it considers to be most important. The architect's design will often depend on it. True, the architect needs a reasonably free hand for setting out the design, but a few major pronouncements by the board will go a long way toward obtaining the facility desired.

Numerous illustrations could be given regarding preferences expressed by different boards—each resulting in distinctly contrasting design solutions to basically similar problems. In one locality, the board requested "a building with a large front toward the main traffic artery, so the taxpayers who drive by can see they are getting their money's worth." In another locality, the board viewed the school as becoming "the center, or hub, of community activity," and in still another situation a desire was expressed for "a view capturing the wooden surroundings, but with ease of maintenance of building above all else." Perhaps the most astounding effect of board consensus on the outcome was the directive to make the building a model for redevelopment of the downtown area. It is from expressions such as these that the design will evolve to an identifiable extent.

The message for the board is to have a clearly defined and appropriate direction for the project, and above all else to keep the main purpose of the educational facility in mind. Thorough planning, as with budgeting, is essential for best results over the long pull.

Chapter 6

Measuring Institutional Strength

The controlling board that takes its assignment seriously will at some point in time direct attention to assessing the strength of the school or college it represents. The duty of the board to remain vigilant in detecting weaknesses, to look for indications of declining strength, and to bolster the organization where needed must receive appropriate attention. Probably no other area of responsibility holds implications as broadly significant as this one.

While the duties of boards have changed little over the years, the uncertainties and potentialities of emerging, unstable times can be extraordinarily challenging. Being heard more and more are concerns about escalating costs in the face of declining standards. How to maintain viable operations in the years ahead, if conditions continue as now developing, may confront authorities everywhere and at every level of education.

The strength, or health, of an organization is an indicator of its capacity to achieve purposes and to withstand adverse conditions when they develop. A healthy school will have the wherewithal to offset the effects of declining or burgeoning enrollments, for example, while those less strong may be unable to continue in similar circumstances without radically altering purposes or practices. The possibilities are not hypothetical. Much evidence of a near crisis already exists. In collegiate ranks, numbers of private liberal-arts colleges are implementing career-oriented programs in order to attract enough enrollees to keep their doors open. Public schools are also coming under fire. In several instances, the doors are being closed in midterm for lack of ability to finish the school year. The bottom line is financial exigency.

This chapter identifies six areas which could lead to failure. A board would be remiss if it made no effort to detect the danger signals early on. It would be incredibly incompetent if it did nothing about the signals when observed.

Strength is a condition of fundamental importance for an educational enterprise. A strong organization can weather crises and achieve quality in its offerings. However, institutional strength does not assure institutional quality. All elements of strength can be present without the right chemistry for putting the resources to use most successfully. Therein lies a board's duty. Every board has an unavoidable stake in producing the proper environment and providing for its effective management.

As a partial solution to problems confronting local school systems, some communities are turning to open-enrollment opportunities for their secondary students. This practice provides at least some freedom of choice by permitting students to enroll in schools outside assigned district boundaries. At the same time, it tends to force the schools to improve the quality of their offerings to remain competitive. Quality and strength are thereby becoming a concern for public schools similarly to that which has existed for years among independent schools and institutions of higher education.

Basically, an institution's strength derives from its resources. Results, and the capacity to continue to achieve favorable results, are as validly related to quality of resources as to the input and process criteria commonly applied in education. Too often assessment is attempted by concentrating only on subjective ratings of such things as the personal traits of staff and faculty. As will be seen, there are better measures of evaluation available.

Establishing Purposes

The development of criteria for measuring strength proceeds from the purposes of the institution. This point bears emphasizing. The basic purpose of any educational institution, whether elementary, secondary, or post secondary, is to provide an effective setting for learning. In simplistic terms, if another setting would be better for the students, then the institution has not been as effective as it should be. In all probability, most institutions will have some outstanding features and some in need of improvement or remedial effort.

The concept of *purposeful learning* applies here. Associated with this concept is the idea that each organization has a utilitarian purpose. All schools and colleges have such, whether stated or not. Several widely applied purposes are: transmitting the culture; preparing youth for vocational and professional pursuits; meeting local, state, and national goals; developing the whole person; instilling appreciation of and preparing for democratic participation; and meeting the needs of society. Although other useful purposes could be listed, these examples suffice to point out the kinds of statements often identified for primary emphasis. Other purposes may be given secondary status.

The complete set of purposes forms the basis for determining the quality and nature of the resources needed. The relationship is readily observed. A school emphasizing instruction in the arts will have physical plant resources different from one emphasizing vocational skills. A high school stressing physical education will employ faculty with backgrounds different from one choosing to excel in the sciences. A college excelling in research needs financial resources different from another concentrating on general education. And so on. Only after the purposes have been clearly defined can the measurement of strength logically occur.

Defining Essentials

To be effective, the determination of strength involves an analysis of the essentials for making the setting for learning all it is intended to be. The primary necessity for learning to occur is *students*. The other essentials may be classified as *services*, *facilities*, *personnel*, *finances*, and *management*. All are measurable resources.

The six essentials are described briefly below. While they are applicable throughout education, they must be interpreted by different criteria of measurement at the several levels.

Services. Students attend a school or college for its services, that is, the activities, both curricular and extracurricular, which are the substance of the learning experience. Purposeful learning could not occur without substance. Further, the variety and quality of offerings are indicators of strength. Where free selection of services exists, as in colleges and some secondary schools, the offerings can have a substantial effect on enrollment. Strong services of certain kinds can easily be shown to attract student clientele, but weak services will often be forced out because of insufficient numbers of interested participants.

Facilities. A physical setting—the buildings, equipment, materials, and surroundings—has become an accepted necessity for effectively and economically instructing students in collective fashion. The adequacy, quality, and condition of these facilities are important, because the environment can facilitate or impede learning significantly. Color and lighting are among the factors known to have a profound effect on learning.

Personnel. In order to learn most effectively, students need direction. Traditionally, this meant teachers and books. Today it is still that, but innovative uses of mentors, television, computers, video tapes, and a large variety of other instructional aids are in vogue. The essential ingredient remains *people*, the faculty and support personnel who carry out the educational plan. Students need the wisdom and direction of competent, mature people above all else.

Finances. Money, often much of it, is fundamental. It is without a doubt often in short supply. Consequently, money is frequently the first apparent indicator of weakness or impending difficulty within the operation.

Management. Contrary to beliefs held by some operatives, management by persons other than themselves must occur for an operation of any complexity to be effective. The people in control and their abilities for planning, organizing, implementing, and evaluating activities are among the determinants of strength and weakness. The quality of the management team will determine how well operational elements are brought together.

Students. As previously indicated, students are the basic resource. Without them nothing else is needed. The ability to recruit and hold them in sufficient numbers is critical for colleges and schools functioning in a free market environment. The size of the student population can be crucial for schools serving a legally defined territory, also. The mere magnitude of student numbers and whether they are increasing or decreasing in magnitude may represent a strengthening or weakening of the basic foundation. Every institution must attain a certain critical mass of students in order to achieve quality and variety in its services, as well as excellence among groups targeted for graduation.

Developing Criteria

Sound, insightful analysis is contingent upon the applicability of evaluative criteria to local situations. While the elements of strength remain the same from place to place, the criteria for making specific evaluations could vary considerably. Public colleges, unlike many high schools, operate very much according to controlled free-enterprise influences, and private colleges operate even more so than public ones in a pure free-enterprise market. Cognizance of this fact and its impact can be extremely important for an authority operating in a competitive environment. The ability to identify and assess the competition may be the determining factor in a college's survival during periods of declining enrollment.

Public school administrators and boards usually have to be concerned about the transporting and truancy of students and, to a lesser extent, about competing with other schools for clients. However, as has been suggested this situation could change with the advent of competition through open enrollment in the secondary schools. Local factors, such as size of the service district or area served, could also dictate the use of criteria peculiar to the situation.

Another consideration when developing measures of strength pertains to the objectivity of the evidence used in evaluating each criterion. Subjective evaluations leave much to be desired. An evaluation of a superintendent's or president's management style by an employees' organization may result in high marks for the executive who never dismisses anyone, yet that administrator may well create serious organizational weaknesses because of the condoning attitude for which he or she has been judged so favorably. Much the better measures of managerial strength are found in the specificity of organizational achievements and results.

The preferred approach to assessment is to compile data according to the criteria set forth and then to make comparisons of performance, internally and externally. Internal comparisons might be made of the year-to-year achievements and aggregate test scores of graduates of the institution. Such measures as a school's investment in its library, its variety academically, and its room utilization ratios are most meaning-ful when compared to external standards promulgated by a state agency responsible for education and the achievements of other schools of like kind. Logically, the comparative data will be compiled by the chief administrator with the assistance of staff for presentation to the board for final analysis.

Criteria pertaining to students, services, finances, facilities, personnel, and management are presented in the Appendix as they might be used in an actual analysis. The criteria are particularly useful to colleges as listed, but with a bit of ingenuity, they can be changed to suit other institutions. The value of an application of any kind will be enhanced if data are compared over time and plotted for trends.

Understanding of the criteria might be enhanced by a brief explanation of the section on students. An analysis of strength in this area centers on five considerations: diversity of clientele, enrollment stability, constituency demand, program specialization, and market factors. Again, these considerations are intended for institutions not populated by compulsory attendance. Thus a private, proprietary, or postsecondary institution having a diverse clientele would be better constituted to withstand a decline in attendance by one student group than could another which serves that one segment of the population alone. Similarly, an institution offering something unique, a popular specialty not readily available elsewhere, has a built-in demand factor for its services. Careful review of the criteria will reveal other significant elements.

Many of the criteria listed or that might be developed for assessing institutional strength are similar in some respects to those contained in self-evaluation instruments made for purposes of accreditation by a nationally recognized body. For that reason, the topics are widely applicable. Every school and college must have students and faculty in adequate numbers to carry out its mission effectively. It needs educational services of appropriate variety and depth for the students, and it needs sufficient finances for keeping the operation going. Lastly, it needs effective management for organizing the enterprise for ongoing goal achievement. How ably the board and top-level administrators develop measures for determining their institution's strength will also serve as an indication of their ability to look ahead and control their institution's future.

Measuring with an Instrument

An instrument can be readily constructed for rating the six essential elements of strength. A scale for this purpose accompanies the sample criteria listed in Appendix A. Each criterion should be rated individually, with an overall evaluation being applied to each group and the institution on the whole. Thorough, factual evidence will be helpful when applying the scale.

Not only does evaluating with an instrument point up areas needing improvement or revision, it also instills in those who do the evaluating a more thorough understanding of the institution. The process may be time-consuming at first, but there is no better way to gain specific knowledge about the institution and the areas needing attention.

Creating Demand

While colleges and schools of all kinds can profit from the suggestions stated in the preceding sections, this section applies mainly to those not acquiring students entirely through mandatory enrollment. This may exclude many public secondary and elementary schools, although those offering classes for adults and those adopting open enrollment practices for teenagers can gain from this subject, too. Any form of enrollment that occurs in competition with other attractions, whatever they may be, could be credited to the demand factor.

Those competing for students have a good chance of remaining strong and able to continue to offer quality education if they have a history of growth (demand maximizing utilization), attract a diverse clientele, offer something unique, remain responsive to demands for various kinds of services, have an excellent placement record among graduates, provide advantages of cost and proximity, effectively practice responsive governance, and have the fiscal soundness necessary for sustaining the operation during periods of adversity. The reasons are considerable and bear reviewing. Diversity of client groups operates as a buffer against possible aberrations in attendance by a single group. One or more highly promoted, highly visible, unique programs of study which are not conveniently accessible elsewhere strengthens the demand. Low tuition and nearness of services have an acknowledged effect on attendance, and a fiscal structure with provisions for contingencies helps to assure the continuation of services in good and bad times. Responsiveness to demands for services, like the prospect of employment upon graduation, creates even more interest among potential enrollees. Of equal importance is the ability of management to anticipate and to plan for contingencies.

Institutions operated in an environment of open enrollment and free choice must be managed in a way that creates demand. The nature, variety, cost, accessibility, and awareness of services are the elements to be controlled. The better the publicity the better the public awareness. The more services offered the more people attracted. The more accessible the services the more students enrolled. The more students enrolled the more special services that can be offered and the lower the costs can be held, thereby creating even greater demand. To an extent, these interrelationships exist wherever free-market principles operate.

During periods of inflation, there occurs a concomitant, virtually self-defeating relationship between enrollment and the financial needs of colleges and schools in a competitive market. In order to offset the effects of rising costs, the additional revenue can be obtained one of three, or a combination of three, ways: (1) increased enrollment, (2) increased fee levels, and (3) additional bequests, government funding, or taxes. The failure of external sources to supply the capital usually results in higher fees for courses.

The effect of higher fees is to deplete the enrollment pool by eliminating those unable to afford the higher level of tuition. The numbers eliminated from the pool represent a loss in income which might have to be compensated for by raising fees even further. Unfortunately, this loss is likely to occur not only among a public generally well-off but also among the population that opts for greater participation in education when economic times are not good. The loss to society when these uncounted numbers remain missing from the roles of educated persons has implications which, though of great importance, remains beyond the immediate purpose of this topic.

Assigning Responsibility

Whatever the type of institution, the controlling board has an obligation to know how well it is performing. Otherwise it operates in a veritable vacuum. Apparently few boards conduct appraisals in an organized manner. Each, along with the chief executive, should define measures for determining institutional strength agreeable to both, and the executive officer should then be held accountable for periodically producing information necessary for the evaluation.

The factors defined here—the quantity and quality of services, facilities, personnel, finances, management, and student clientele—are the basic indicators of strength. They must be analyzed and applied according to institutional type and mission.

Chapter 7

Working With Management

Institutional progress is contingent upon solidarity in the relationship between the board and its administrators. A strong administrative team can manage for a while without the support of the board, and a board can occasionally negate an important administrative decision, but a generally supportive, harmonious relationship is essential for success in the long term. Prolonged weakness in the relationship by either party will likely lead to a low-level type of governance and accomplishment.

Both personal and impersonal conditions affect board-management relationships. Impersonal conditions are those related to periods of progress, stability, decline, or crisis resulting from nonhuman factors. They affect operations positively and negatively, with attitudes of authorities changing as markedly as the operational conditions change. The personal conditions of most import are those attendant to the association and interfacing of the authorities. In combination, the several factors can produce a solid foundation for success or, in unfavorable environments, rapid turnover in the executive office.

How a particular relationship develops relates also to the board's realization of the complexity of the executive's leadership role in dealing with various personnel and day-to-day routines. As a rule, a board must support the executive's actions. That support is essential for effective management under virtually all normal circumstances.

Understanding the Times

The problems of the executive office in education are manifold, and an appreciation of them helps in establishing good relations at the top. An executive must often deal with circumstances relevant to retrenchment, participatory government, competitive markets, governmental encroachment, erosion of autonomy, collective bargaining, broad judicial mandate, energy conservation, and affirmative action, as well as the effects of an increased propensity to engage persons in positions of power in litigation for alleged wrongdoing. One or more of these matters added to the customary concerns about finances can make management very complex.

The times are such in education that an astute, prospective superintendent or president will be as concerned about a board's style of operating as about the institution. Information along that line could be crucial. Any offer of employment should be rejected that is extended by a board which has persistently failed to maintain appropriate standards of conduct and performance. Nobody's history should be ignored, and no board should hire an administrator without first making clear its expectations and manner of operating.

Cooperative decision making has gained wide acceptance in education, not only involving administrators and boards but also groups of employees. The concern for appropriate internal consultation and compromise on significant issues has been resoundingly driven home to many an uninitiated administrator.

Certainly, educational leadership no longer remains the prerogative of one person alone. The stereotype of the executive officer as a scholarly and distinguished educator who exercises unchallenged managerial authority has long ago passed from the scene. The historian's description of the educational leader as one wielding great power, making unquestioned decisions, and being revered by everyone also has no place in the modern-day scenario. The constituencies have changed that. Their acceptance of unions in education and the widely held belief in a democratic, participatory mode of governance have effectively lead to the replacement of autocratic executives with facilitative-minded leaders.

The thrust toward faculty and student representation on boards (both voluntary and mandatory among the states) further exemplifies the point. While representing an inherent conflict of interest in one respect, this trend captures the tenor of the times. Giving faculty and students an official voice in determining their own salaries and fees would have been unthinkable not many years ago.

Not everyone admits employees into the decision-making structure, of course. John Silber, currently president of Boston University, contends "the more democratic the university the weaker it becomes." Many would not subscribe to his form of autocracy, but he has unquestionably steered his university away from bankruptcy and enjoys the support of his board for having done so.

Boards and executives are needed who will be firm in defense of their authority so as not to allow complete erosion or serious usurpation of their roles. They have a mandate to govern. Other constituencies can be heard without abdicating to them the power to decide. Employee organizations represent the most powerful groups in some places, yet who holds liability for errors of commission or omission is abundantly clear in, say, affirmative action and for problems such as misuse of funds, inaccurate reporting and contract default. The chief executive remains inadvertently tied to the results of decisions and activities on campus or school grounds whoever initiates them or acts them out. Participation by groups whose interests are not always in concert with the obligations of management could be dangerous. Although there might not be a discernible cause-and-effect relationship in each instance, investigation might reveal significant correlations between the increased power vested in faculty and students and the current decline in academic achievement.

The board's posture is extremely important in this context. A board has a fundamental responsibility to protect the executive's authority to act, to delegate, and to manage. Final authority, the source of authority for the executive, resides with the board of control.

Board functioning, too, has become more complex and demanding. Much pressure for accountability comes from the public. The normal reaction is to explain policies, defend actions, and become involved in operations. The danger is overinvolvement, with sharply contrasting views emerging between board and executive. The applicable rule of order is to leave management to those prepared for it and to defend the propriety of doing so when deemed necessary.

Letting Administrators Manage

A simplistic differentiation of roles commonly stated in literature on the subject holds the board responsible for setting policy and the chief administrator obligated to implement it. In actuality no discrete differentiation can be made. Considerable overlapping occurs between policy making and management. Because of this lack of clarity, overextension by the board into the management of internal affairs sometimes occurs. Only a benignly passive executive officer permits that to happen without protest, though, preferably, through subtle persuasion.

Ordinarily having few experts in education among their numbers, board members must rely on the executive officer and staff to identify issues and apply policy internally. There are cases on record, nonetheless, where boards have misinterpreted obligations and their capabilities by becoming entrenched in administration. Although instances occur where pliable administrators allow forays into their territory to continue unrestrained, by and large the propensity of boards to dabble excessively in operational management is an acknowledged complaint among administrators.

Board committees are especially prone to function in a managerial capacity. Some superimpose their judgment by dictating operational regulations, and some bypass the administration when working with employees. The unfortunate tendency is to pursue details outside the policy-making area. The welfare of the institution can best be furthered if the board requires its committees to give reasoned reflective consideration to the larger issues of mission, philosophy, goals, development, progress, and assessment.

In place of healthy, constructive, cooperative planning and action, a committee's involvement sometimes interferes with managerial duties. Members, eager to be helpful, often accept committee work as the vehicle. A capable chairperson will do what he or she can to prohibit any interference or untenable duplication. Without explicit direction, the timeworn adage about effort expended varying inversely as the importance of the action could hold true.

A board should not attempt to manage an institution except in the rarest of circumstances. Administrators, including poor ones, cannot logically be held accountable for operations if their managerial duties and authority have been taken over. Poor management should be improved or the administrators replaced.

Delegating Authority

Delegation is an act of understanding and confidence. Board members need not try to manage internal affairs. They seldom have the foundation or the opportunity to interface consistently in operational activities as do full-time administrators. Mutually defined roles should address this issue, with the executive being given authority to act expeditiously in the absence of a specific policy.

With delegation, extreme care should be exercised to balance authority with responsibility. Responsibility in excess of authority leads to feelings of frustration and impotence among subordinates. Contrarily, the board loses control if authority is delegated without restraint. Open and frank discussion of the matter can be useful in maintaining an appropriate balance. This might be done at an annual retreat.

Clarifying Roles

The potential for conflict over roles can be diminished by setting out clarifying statements in a guide or memorandum of understanding. Explicit agreement on all points is essential. Conscientiously developed, the document attempts to curtail overlapping of duties in areas where conflict might occur.

Figure 7.1 (page 76) contains a few statements of the kind helpful in establishing an understanding of the respective roles of board and executives. Although not shown in the example, responsibilities could be listed under topics such as general policy, budget and finance, facilities, student services, educational program, personnel, governance and management, communication and information, and evaluation. Subtopics on this order focus attention on specific areas when creating the memorandum of understanding.

Differentiations such as those presented here can be helpful in avoiding duplicity or involvement in operational detail. Some statutes contribute to the difficulty in making a distinction by assigning certain managerial responsibilities to boards. For instance, legislation in one state expressly requires boards to submit financial reports to a state agency. The board must recognize in those situations the difference between assigned accountability and responsibility for delegating and doing. Operations must be left to the staff positioned for the purpose. The board monitors the results.

Sharing Responsibility

While a board and its executive are not equal partners, the best situation develops where they perform in a shared relationship. Ultimate authority in the public sector resides with the board. That is the law. Nevertheless, an astute one listens carefully to its administrative staff. Responsibility and liability shared relative to affirmative

Board's Duties	Executive's Duties
□Adopt policy in the best interest of the institution	□Recommend for adoption only justifiable policies
□Accept recommendations only from the executive officer	□Seek input from subordinates but make final decisions and recommendations
□Require annual financial audits and review results	□Schedule external audits and submit results
□Evaluate institutional progress and quality	□Suggest criteria for the assessment
□Stay out of negotiations with employees	□Meet with employees or delegate as feasible
□Ignore or refer to the executive and allegation or rumor	□Respond to the chair or board after investigating and preparing a response

Figure 7.1 Differentiating Board-Executive Responsibilities

action and collective bargaining especially exemplify the need for a close working arrangement. Loyalty, support, and compliance by the administration are no less expected, since the board's control extends throughout the organization.

Both failures and successes become mutually assignable when responsibility is shared. Historically, boards have rarely looked to themselves for fault when something went wrong. They have often looked for a new executive, instead.

Sharing, counseling, open communication, candid appraisal, and conscientious performance of duties provide an environment for a supportive and trusting board-executive relationship. In this context the executive assists the board in performing its function, and the board never meets alone or acts without a recommendation by the executive—the exception being when evaluating that person's performance. Frequent consultation becomes the preferred method of operating. Although both parties may have to adjust gradually to this interactive role, together they can create an atmosphere of frankness and candor in which all members of the board sense their participation is truly wanted.

Positive results are not always easily attained. The problem may be one of extremes. At one level, there is a distinct ornamentality among the members. Some members will sit back silently at meetings because they feel unable to match the preparation and staff work by professionals who put on a show when presenting a proposal. Members with misguided notions about their expertise represent another extreme, sometimes substituting their judgment for that of better qualified professionals. The care and feeding of the board can become a difficult task for the executive and chairperson in severe situations like those.

Any expectation of total harmony in board-executive dealings is unrealistic, but solidarity and agreement on important issues must be present. Boards split politically or philosophically may have difficulty pulling together to support an administrative position. Particularly bad is the situation where part of the membership sides with a pressure group instead of keeping the welfare of students and institution uppermost. Adversities of this nature can often be avoided if the chairperson will call for an executive session (when permissible) in which the executive is asked to lead a discussion of relevant facts and possible consequences of various actions.

Nurturing Trust

Trust is essential in a successful relationship. Professionals in positions of leadership must have the honest, open support and encouragement of their superiors. The person who believes an employee will be most productive when kept on edge and uncertain about a superior's attitude toward his or her work operates under a false assumption. Administrators cannot work at peak efficiency when threatened, even by subtle inference. Some are cautiously sensitive as it is. They usually know of the plethora of entrapments awaiting them as managers and of their vulnerability as targets for blame when actions do not occur to a group's liking. The board which shifts blame, offers public criticism, or otherwise engages in condescending and confrontational behavior toward the executive further diminishes opportunities for achieving the lasting confidence needed.

By virtue of their position, one or two members of a board can do much either to destroy or nurture feelings of trust. They can publicly display attitudes which range anywhere from outright recrimination to respectful admiration. They can believe anything whispered in a negative vein, promptly accuse the executive of incompetence, malfeasance, misfeasance, or nonfeasance, or they can reserve judgment until all facts of an issue are known. They can pursue a course of harassment, embarrassment, clandestine investigation, and displacement of the executive by operating from an office on campus, or they can allow none of those things to happen. The choices are manifold. Undoubtedly, more than one good administrator has resigned for reasons of a poor choice.

Trust works the other way, too. An executive's failure to implement an unpopular policy, coupled with criticism in public of the board's action, does not contribute as desired. Executives are obligated to apply and support policy without disagreement, whether they had expressed opposition originally or not. There is no room to compromise on this point.

Strong statements of admonishment like these should in no way be construed to mean friendship has no place among members and their executive officer. Friendships should be encouraged, and social functions are not out of bounds. Nevertheless, friendly relations must not be allowed to overshadow the professional, businesslike demeanor so basic to unbiased action.

Of the ways to develop trust, one that stands out has to do with a supportive posture between board and executive in areas of deficiency. Each strives to compensate for the other's weaknesses. Neither boards nor administrators are always correct in their decisions and actions, just as infallible judgment is not one of man's virtues. Trite though the solution may seem, a mutually supportive attitude, good will, diplomacy, and a cooperative stance can go a long way toward offsetting the shortcomings.

Supporting the Chief Executive

Support, a key element in fostering trust, is necessary for successfully managing an educational institution. Anyone reasonably observant knows there are likely to be unavoidable instances which make the official's job difficult. When a detraction does occur, a strong board will stand firm with its executive.

Individuals who have conversed much with colleagues or read much literature on the subject are aware of both admirable and horrendous stories about how differently boards have reacted to attacks on their executive officer. Some boards have exhibited commendable courage, decency, and common sense by defending the executive's innocence unless proven otherwise. Some have seen through the motives of noisy detractors and publicly denounced such tactics. Others have been pathetically timid. Some, being more afraid of having their personal images tarnished than of preserving the good of the institution, have quickly dismissed their executive in hopes of placing blame and simultaneously hiding their own inadequacies, and some have remained naively silent in the face of unfounded charges, evidently being without compassion or awareness of how their inaction could erode leadership effectiveness. A few have appropriately dismissed their chief official on proper evidence.

The mettle of a board becomes evident, particularly, when storms of unionization and collective bargaining are fomenting. At those times employees may become militant adversaries. An aggressive tactic is to attack a major figure in the free press. If a group of employees forces the executive out of office by this tactic, one can surely expect the group will work harmoniously thereafter only with those who do what they like. Unless the board speaks out in opposition to the attack, any strong leader who occupies the post or who would take the job in replacement could expect similar treatment later. Employees should no more be allowed to select their superintendent or president by this means (or any other for that matter) than should a board hand-pick the head of the employees' union.

An analysis of why officials in charge of schools and colleges in the public sector have come under attack so frequently in recent times reveals interesting but unfortunate reasons. One reason is a general assertiveness for individual rights in the context of affirmative action, equal employment opportunity, due process, etc., which automatically puts the chief executive in a defensive role. Another factor is that public figures are not accorded the same protection by law in matters of libel and slander as are citizens generally. Hence, vocal critics take little risk when speaking out against those in positions of leadership.

Former university president Herman B Wells astutely summarized the executive's needs. He referred to college presidents, specifically. "Needed," Wells said, "is to be born with the physical stamina of a Greek athlete, the cunning of a Machiavelli, the wisdom of a Solomon, the courage of a lion, if possible—but above all, the stomach of a goat." Wells, of course, had considerable experience as an educational leader.

One of the most serious mistakes a board can make is to allow students or employees to circumvent administrative channels when airing their concerns. When a group has been permitted to meet with the board before consulting with their supervisors and higher level administrators, the board members assume the role of managers. A precedent exists for still more bypassing. Eventually, some alert member will realize the board has neither the time nor the special education for operating in that role. Hopefully this would happen early on. Otherwise the executive might consider resigning, if that has not already been done, for thereafter extreme difficultly could be encountered when attempting to regain the respect and control the office must command.

While executives should be relied on for knowledge of institutional affairs, the ultimate power of decision which resides with the board derives from the idea that members are guardians of good who have not become tainted by internal interests. Boards sometimes misrepresent this strength. They expect the executive to function as an obedient follower of their wishes instead of a professional leader of the organization. Confrontation instead of cooperation easily results in those situations.

How far should a board go in supporting its chief executive? Certainly, any appointee who demonstrates critical, repeated mishandling of affairs should be terminated, but dismissal should not occur as long as he or she does what is expected or makes reasonable progress toward that end. Executives do not ordinarily become incompetent overnight. Ample time usually exists for corrective action when needed. If a termination does become imminent, however, the use of public exposure and pressure through the press to achieve it is blatantly unethical.

Every board should consider defining the support it is prepared to extend in exchange for good management and progress toward the goals to which it has agreed. That support may be moral, financial, or legal. A knowledgeable official will appreciate those considerations under nearly all circumstances.

Handling Allegations

Allegations about officials take many forms, varying from sheer rumor to written resolutions seeking dismissal. The instances are common enough to caution an uninitiated board to be aware. "Hate" letters, often written to the chairperson by a probationary employee, and "no confidence" resolutions, usually drafted by faculty and submitted to the press, represent the charges made short of litigation. Efforts to force an administrator to resign through intimidation or to pressure the board to dismiss the employee are known to occur at all levels.

How a board handles accusations and complaints may depend on how prepared it is for the eventuality. Boards sometimes overreact by ordering an immediate investigation. Resignation of the accused is the likely result. Only an exceptionally strong leader will survive an investigation, whether guilty or not, and probably very few administrators would want to remain at a place where the accuser's word appears to carry more weight than that of the accused. Malcontents, and there are those among employees in many organizations, will seize upon the opportunity with spiteful vengeance. Whether the board conducts a clandestine search behind closed doors or a consultant is hired to interrogate employees makes little difference. The results are likely to be the same. They generally support the supposition that "if you want to be rid of an official, simply conduct an investigation of his or her operation."

Controlling bodies have a more rational, more ethical course available to them. First, as has been said, the accused person should be treated as being innocent until proven guilty. Second, the board should emphatically and summarily dismiss any accusation which has no substance. Third, the board should promptly relate charges or accusations to the one accused. Fourth, the board should provided the person adequate time to study the situation, develop a position, and respond to the allegation. An official might be able to resolve the problem him- or herself, if the board reiterates its support. The board that does nothing appears to be neutral (perhaps uncertain), with the administrator left to struggle alone. This posture may achieve results under certain conditions, but it is most certainly not justified when a charge is leveled in connection to the dismissal of an incompetent employee or the implementation of board policy.

Exactly how each situation might be handled depends on circumstances. A statement of finality carefully drawn by the chairperson in a letter to the accuser, a succinct, direct comment at a board meeting, or a firm response through the press will usually suffice. Some allegations, of course, should not be dignified by a public response, and that may be the way to address a reporter's inquiry. In general, personnel problems should be left to the executive to resolve as a matter of prudence, provided the board makes known at the appropriate time that it backs final resolution by the executive officer.

Votes of "no confidence" in an administrator frequently receive wide coverage, with regional newspapers, television, and radio publicizing the matter. Only a woefully uninformed board will be impressed. Many aggressive groups (usually faculty) have threatened to unionize or strike unless certain incumbents are removed from office, only to carry out the threat after their board capitulated on the first demand.

Cases are on record where the response has been notably decisive. In one instance, a board completely ended efforts by a dissident group to undermine their superintendent when the chairperson denounced the tactics in an open letter to the entire community of employees. In another, a board had the accusers individually face the accused. The board members, after listening to the accusers' apologies and observing the tears of regret—the accusers where not then in view of their peers—voted unanimously to extend the contract of this embattled college president. The net result was reinforcement of authority and control.

Addressing Board Critics

Clearly, not all attacks are directed toward the administration. Boards receive their share of criticism. Students, faculty, legislators, and citizens in the community are among the categories of people who have sought the resignation of full boards. Faculty organizations, often in conjunction with a threat to strike over salaries, are particularly inclined to vent their wrath on the controlling body.

An able board will not equivocate under pressure of criticism, but it will exercise initiative and speak out courageously in justifiable defense. Its response will be restrained, both for tactical and for legal reasons. Verbal confrontations can seldom be won in a public forum, and little is to be gained by engaging in a shouting contest. The best advice is to counter the attack with firmness, decorum, and sophistication—never capitulating from weakness. The chairperson should be the board's designate for responding. The executive might also offer a comment in support, and legal counsel might be consulted when evaluating the efficacy of a reply.

Stimulating a Weak Board

Weakness in a controlling body is anathematic to institutional progress. Heaven help the executive who has one. He or she may persevere for a while in a state of frustration, but at some point in time that unfortunate person will probably quit in despair or succumb from the punishment received because of the absence of support.

Boards are entitled to the glory of accomplishment, provided they do not shirk responsibilities when the going becomes difficult. Weak ones have been observed avoiding duties at the first sign of controversy in order to keep names of members out of the newspapers and to diminish possibilities of a personal reputation being blemished. Weak boards do not often admit they are weak, nor do they resign. If challenged, they will rationalize their failure to take a firm stand on important issues. The executive who can survive the invidious scrambling to avoid every threatening issue that arises in an era of collective bargaining is nothing short of a miracle worker.

A chairperson or strong member can hold a board on course. Situations emerge where either one can exert more influence on the group than can the executive. One person alone, if persuasive enough, can prevent others from selling out to forceful adversaries in false hope of buying respect and cooperation. Potentially most damaging are unofficial conciliatory statements relative to salary negotiations, collective bargaining, and grievance proceedings.

The best the ordinary chief administrative officer can do is to work behind the scenes, encouraging members to prepare for uncomfortable eventualities, to recognize responsibilities, and to build courage for maintaining control and preserving authority. Every opportunity must be used to do that. The annual in-service workshop might not be opportunity enough.

Scheduling an Annual Retreat

An annual retreat, or workshop, can be invaluable in improving performance. It affords an opportunity for board and executive to meet to discuss how to improve upon past practices in preparation for the future. Open, honest, and friendly interchange must be the order of proceedings to establish rapport. No one should neglect attending the complete session by the excuse of insufficient time to do so. All board members must be resigned to fulfill the time demands, or they should seek another less demanding avocation. The direction given the institution is much too crucial to be left to those who do not pursue efforts which hold promise of improving governance and, hence, institutional progress.

The annual "get away" will be most beneficial if it is held before a major crisis or misunderstanding develops. A proactive, rather than a reactive, style should dominate. Any reluctance to take part might be overcome by the chair emphasizing the need for everyone's attendance and participation. A spot away from distractions of the workplace has advantages for meetings of this kind.

The retreat provides a good forum for discussing administrative accountability. While no board should attempt to manage, there must be concern about managerial excellence. In order to appraise the executive's performance properly, objective measures of evaluation are needed. These are treated in detail in the next chapter.

Chapter 8

Evaluating Administrative Performance

An effectively functioning board of control evaluates performance of three types: its own, the institution's, and the employees'. An assessment of institutional performance can be completed through a careful analysis of strengths and weaknesses as recommend in Chapter 6. Determining how effectively the board itself performs is the subject of Chapter 9. The performance of employees, specifically the effectiveness of administrators, receives treatment from the board's viewpoint in the topics which follow.

The board has an extremely important role in personnel evaluation. It holds responsibility for having evaluations completed internally at each level as a means of determining organizational effectiveness and assuring progress toward established goals. It fulfills its duty best by evaluating the chief executive and holding that officer accountable for implementing procedures for evaluating other employees within the system.

The primary concern of an authority responsible for evaluating personnel should be their productivity, while recognizing that the measures to be applied in education are different from those commonly used in the profit-making sector. Administrators should be evaluated thoroughly and systematically in that light, but none should held singularly accountable for responsibilities shared within the organization. The authority and accompanying academic freedom accorded faculty as a body, by tradition, law, and regulation, signifies an essential difference between educational organizations and other forms of enterprise. Good management necessitates the use of a process of appraisal designed for the employees of the particular organization.

Establishing a Philosophy of Evaluation

Personnel undergo formal evaluations for purposes of (1) determining needed improvement and (2) determining conditions of employment such as pay, promotion, and retention. Administrators, being in prominent positions, should be evaluated as thoroughly and frequently as anyone else. The conscientious ones will insist on that being done.

Every administrator holds undelegable responsibility for evaluating the performance of subordinates supervised and for making applicable recommendations to superiors. Mid-management officers hold responsibility for reviewing and altering, rejecting, or supporting recommendations of first-line supervisors prior to their submission to the appointing authority—the chief executive and/or board of control—in whom final decision-making authority has been vested. Those responsibilities have been and continue to be the essence of organizational control and the inherent duty of management as a means of assuring institutional progress and vitality. Organizational direction and control are the very reason for administrators, administrative authority, and organizational management. Thus, personnel evaluation remains a prerogative of management within the formal administrative structure.

The philosophy underlying this position is premised on recognition of the need for personnel with expertise in different areas. Faculty are employed to teach, classified employees are hired to provide skills in support of professional staff, and administrators are placed under contract to direct employees' actions within the framework of policy and goals. The managerial component maintains control through a system of hierarchial direction and evaluation.

A hierarchial system does not preclude using informal evaluations by colleagues for purposes of self-improvement. Certainly, input may be sought at lower levels, but those assessments should not become the dictating source of authority. Should subordinates gain the privilege of passing judgment on their supervisors (a practice tantamount to workers selecting their bosses), the authority vested in management for employing and retaining personnel who maximize organizational goal achievement could be irretrievably eroded.

The possible consequences of systemwide assessments by peers and subordinates for purposes of determining pay, promotion, and tenure can be counterproductive. The practice might actually produce nothing worthy of commendation.

In one known situation, the practice reached truly ridiculous proportions. Faculty were accorded authority for evaluating administrators in their respective departments, and all employees were required to evaluate their peers and supervisors. Normally directed evaluations (supervisors to employees) lost impact. Personnel became apprehensively tense, as everyone seemed to be evaluating almost everyone else in sight. Evaluations inclined toward popularity contests. Many employees gave ratings on others about whom they had very limited knowledge relative to duties, responsibilities, and performance; segments of faculty effectively chose department heads who would make the least demands on them by down-rating those conscientious about accountability; and institutional goals were practically ignored, as each group had no strong leadership to work by. The unfortunate concomitants were continual internal dissension and turmoil, eventually unionization and strikes by faculty, and the ultimate loss of some purpose and quality throughout the system. Not all peer and subordinate evaluations could be expected to precipitate the undesirable consequences that this one had, but the potential for experiencing some adverse consequences would seem to be present wherever similar applications occur.

Persons favoring a system in which subordinates evaluate their superiors would do well to recognize that many of the duties and activities of administrators simply are not visible throughout the institution. Faculty and staff generally occupy positions too far distant from the interworkings of higher offices to have more than an iota of a notion as to how effective their leaders perform with the legislature, governmental bureaucracies, other external agencies, and the board. Neither do they fully know of the alternative choices available to top management and of the lengthy, detailed, behind-the-scenes foundation work on which decision making, progressive leadership, long-range planning, and future developments depend. They can only offer perceptions, and probably speciously contrived ones at that.

The controlling board which insists on administrators being evaluated by subordinates (anonymously, of course) should accept similar evaluations of itself. In all probability, doing that would result in many more resignations among boards than have been experienced to date. This result might be good in some instances, but it is much more likely to have negative consequences over the long term. The potential for the board being pressured to relinquish essential controls in order to appease the evaluators and avoid unfavorable assessments should not be dismissed out of hand. Some board members are already too sensitive to attitudes of faculty and staff. Why exacerbate the problem?

Members of a body as important as an educational board must not base judgments on emotional appeal, and they must resist tendencies toward unobjective influences from whatever source. Like administrators, boards must not be influenced by subtle and overly coercive pressures to please. Their leadership effectiveness depends on an aptly applied rationality, which an evaluation system harboring elements of a popularity poll could utterly destroy.

Adopting Policy Guidelines

Whatever its underlying philosophy, each board should prepare and have published a policy on the subject of personnel evaluation. The policy might merely charge the executive officer with developing and implementing a comprehensive system. In any event, specific criteria and procedural guidelines should be put in place in all units of the organization.

Sample guidelines for evaluating employees at various levels are set forth in the following statements:

1.　The board of control evaluates the chief executive officer. Unless specifically delegated, the board maintains final authority relative to results of formal evaluations of all other personnel.

2.　The chief executive officer is responsible for evaluating employees reporting directly to him or her, for reviewing recommendations on all other employees, and for making final recommendations to the board in matters of employment or pay.

3.　Other administrators and staff are responsible for evaluating employees reporting directly to them, for reviewing and evaluating subordinate supervisors' recommendations, if any, and for submitting defensible recommendations to the next higher supervising authority.

4.　All employees shall be evaluated annually, with progress reviews scheduled at least semiannually.

5.　Evaluation techniques, instruments, and procedures shall be reviewed and approved throughout higher administrative levels, with an effort made to develop a fair process through employee input at appropriate levels.

6.　Evaluations by peers, subordinates, and students shall not be used in the officially sanctioned system of evaluation, promotion, and retention.

Employees should be apprised of the specific points to be covered in the evaluation. The board's appraisal of the chief administrator is no exception. Full information and understanding at the beginning of the period for which the evaluation is planned are requisite to acceptance and compliance.

Applying a Fundamental Rule

Generally, the evaluation of the chief administrator is one of a board's most difficult tasks. A noteworthy problem is the members' limited experience. Rarely has a whole board become skilled in evaluating others for purposes of improvement, promotion, or termination. Of those newly seated on the board, probably very few will have ever before held the fate of chief executive at their discretion, and probably fewer still will have acquired prior experience in passing such judgment on the executive officer of a school, college, or university. The sum of the previous experience in a given instance could be nil. Yet, the members of a board are the only ones in position to determine properly how well the executive is doing.

How, then, might a board proceed? One should first select a method of evaluation. In the process, all members should try to visualize themselves in the position of their executive officer. The confidence of many could be impressively shaken upon realizing that in the role of executive each member would be reporting to more bosses at one time—the full board—than most had reported to individually throughout all their working years. The gravity of the situation ordinarily increases in times of contract renewal, because the executive's future, his or her family's future, and to an extent the institution's future are affected by the outcome. With conditions as they are, there is a basic rule to be observed: *Never subject anyone to any form of evaluation to which you, the evaluator, would not want to be subjected in similar circumstances.* The rule has a biblical ring to it, but it expresses an extremely important ethic. It urges the evaluator to be scrupulously fair. Nobody wants to submit to unfair treatment in any form.

The executive in an educational organization who fails to insist on an objective, formal evaluation by the board risks catastrophe. The scarcity of carefully designed, reliable systems of review which set out expectations and provide for improvement in needed areas, probably more than anything else, has been the underlying cause of the high rate of turnover among chief educational officers. Off-the-cuff, gut-level assessments have been among the subjective forms of assessment commonly used. Apparently few boards have been educated to the need and procedures for evaluating more effectively.

Avoiding Subjectivity

Objectivity is imperative. Factual, unbiased evidence should be the basis of an evaluation. The use of any rating system which largely depends on personal judgments can be unreliable and even unjust. Subjectively oriented assessments are open, not only to the sound judgments of people, but also to their uninformed opinions, questionable motives, aberrant whims, prejudices, and hearsay.

Board members have a conscionable duty for fairness, and they will usually try to be fair. Therein lies the problem. They are typically called on to express feelings about a person for which all facts for judging fairly are not known.

Subjective rating methods remain popular, nevertheless. Much of their popularity stems from the ease with which the rating scales can be administered and scored, in addition to the minimal effort needed to record perceptions. Their weakness derives from the vagaries inherent in human perceptions. Thoroughly documented is the propensity of observers to perceive a subject differently from one time to the next and according to circumstances unrelated to the situation as perceived. The influence of the rater's background of experience is another phenomenon known to be involved.

The inadequacy of perception scales can be easily shown. A statement taken from an instrument of this type illustrates the point: "Develops initiative among subordinates by delegating challenging tasks." This statement seems noble in concept, but it practically defies measurement. Are we to believe that every subordinate is capable of handling delegated tasks, is free to do so, or that the need to delegate challenging tasks would not lead to "dumping" the difficult ones? Moreover, by what standard is credit given for delegating when the result is poor performance and no evidence of initiative developing? Because of its ambiguities and lack of measurability, this type of statement should be avoided in most applications.

Personal traits scales, social characteristics checklists, descriptive essay procedures, critical incidents records, and structured group or individual interview techniques are among the other systems in use. Most of these represent evaluation at its subjective best. Besides the problems previously alluded to, a major concern is the penchant for emphasizing human relations criteria.

The acceptance of the social or personal relations approach results in part from educational theorists having advanced their ideas about the evaluation process without having been in positions of managerial responsibility long enough to know what emphasis is important. *Getting along with everyone* and *being liked* have gained more importance in some quarters than attaining institutional progress and organizational quality—the primary achievements for which administrators are responsible.

Theorists sometimes espouse a compelling syllogism. It goes this way: Education is a human relations function; administrators are educators; therefore, administrators must be evaluated in a human relations context.

The shortcoming of such reasoning has been sadly demonstrated by a college president who did all possible to compensate faculty at the highest level, because, he rationalized, "a well-paid faculty is a happy faculty." The strong support by faculty was evidence of the way this president implemented his philosophy. His trustees also thought they had an exceptional leader, considering the good rapport established. All went well for several years, that is, until one year when the accumulated effect of his folly left the college's budget at an astonishingly large deficit with nothing in reserve to pay the bill. The president's popularity quickly declined. He and other employees lost their jobs. The irony of the situation was that poor management skills went unattended, perpetrating the most despicable human relations trick of all: the unnecessary loss of jobs and employment.

Several conclusions may be drawn from this case: (1) There is much more to administration than concern about social interaction, (2) perceptions by subordinates do not always truly measure administrative and managerial abilities or worth, (3) a board would be well-advised to tie an administrative evaluation to specific responsibilities, rather than to a system open to the whims of popularity, and (4) an evaluation should serve not only as a means of identifying individual strengths and weaknesses but also as a basis for correcting troublesome areas.

The evaluation of an executive officer should be based systematically and objectively on achievements in relation to duties. Performance and results—not feelings or perceptions of human interaction, social traits, or style of leadership—are the basis for measuring an executive's effectiveness in the all-important area of institutional progress and vitality. Once this fact is understood, the board can establish a valid process. The responsibility shared with the board relative to fulfilling the school or college's mission and attaining goals then becomes the primary area of appraisal.

Knowing the Executive's Needs

An executive needs a comprehensive plan to work by in order to be free from constraints and the uncertainty of not knowing what the board considers important. By having expectations specifically listed, emphasis can then be placed on areas of institutional need and self-improvement. The plan should be endorsed by the full board. It is one of the executive's greatest needs.

The plan should define *everything* the board considers to be important for directing and assessing the chief administrator's performance. A complete document constitutes a contract of understanding which each party has an obligation to follow. The administrator knows exactly what is expected, as there is no latitude for surprises, and the board can measure results against specific expectations and standards. Moreover, the written document provides for continuity of expectations, an especially important matter for the executive at times of turnover and replacement in the board's membership.

Of importance in any system of evaluation is freedom of action. A chief executive must be a risk-taker who, if need be, has courage to act alone. As the caption reads to a picture James B. Conant, former president of Harvard, kept in his office: "Behold the turtle! He makes progress *only* with his neck out." Board members must understand the nature, the subtleties, the uniqueness of the executive's solitary role so that they will allow an occasional mistake.

A mutually designed, reviewed, objective performance evaluation instrument can do much to foster understanding of the executive's role and responsibilities. It will protect against taking spurious action for a single error, but it will also indicate when gross or repeated mismanagement occurs. Periodic feedback from board to executive, provided it is not excessively critical, can be helpful in fulfilling expectations and standards.

The job description provides the criteria to be covered in an evaluation instrument. A complete job description specifies what is to be done; a complete evaluation instrument indicates how well to do it. An executive cannot work effectively without them.

Observing Sound Principles

Every employee needs to know what the boss expects to be accomplished, and those expectations should be made known from the beginning. In that way a deliberate effort can be made to comply and perform as desired. It is perhaps true that the Great American Pastime is telling the other fellow where he went wrong (Public officials everywhere can attest to the veracity of this statement). But it is the evaluator, not the person evaluated, who went wrong if the latter receives criticism while not having been clearly informed of all expectations. An evaluation can proceed in a positive context if the standards of performance have been made known beforehand and relate to the job. Then, the experience seems more likely to be an opportunity for growth than a punitive exercise.

Methods of evaluation are recommended which have these qualities, regardless of who is being evaluated:

1. They emphasize performance, not the person. Results achieved are more important than personal and social traits, which do not necessarily relate to accomplishments.

2. They pertain to the job. Assigned duties and responsibilities within the realm of institutional goals are the reason for the person's employment and are the proper basis for evaluation.

3. They concentrate on measurable outcomes. Criteria and standards of performance are set forth in writing and in terms which discriminate measurably and meaningfully.

4. They are used systematically. Evaluations are formally and periodically applied, with intermittent progress reviews. Possible surprises are avoided by having applicable criteria made known before the period of work to be evaluated begins, and improvement can be expected as a result of occasional feedback.

5. They reflect mutual agreement. The criteria and standards of evaluation have been developed and accepted by both the evaluator and the person to be evaluated.

6. They are applied fairly. Evaluations are performed openly (not anonymously) by those in positions of supervision and higher authority (the board for the executive). Protection against partiality and the biases of a dominating voice can readily occur by following the chain of command.

Although the supervising authority must be sure the employee's performance and evaluations conform to the organization's plans and goals, the employee should be given an opportunity to help set his or her own standards of performance. When so done, the individual will often attempt to set higher goals than would be the case with the supervisor working alone. The standards finally agreed upon must be within the realm of the attainable.

After completing a personal evaluation, the results should be kept confidential. Except in rare legal situations, boards and administrators should restrict detailed information about individual evaluations to normal administrative channels. Both the law of privacy and principles of ethicality are at work here. While public officials do not always enjoy the same legal guarantees of privacy as do other employees, a board in a public organization should be as careful about protecting the confidentiality of its superintendent's or president's rating as it must be for other employees.

Evaluating Objectively

What constitutes an objective appraisal for an executive officer? The preceding list identifies the main features. There can be, however, no such thing as a completely objective system. Some subjectivity will always be present. The emphasis on objectivity becomes the dominant goal. The first requisite is to base the criteria on observable elements in the job, not on personal judgments or perceptions by the one doing the evaluating. As previously stated, the job description forms the foundation around which standards of performance are built.

Standards of performance, properly called *standards of expectation*, should be established mutually by employee and supervising authority, and they should be drawn-up before the period of work begins on which the evaluation will be based. The standards should also be expressed in measurable terms, taking into account the quantity and quality of the work, the amount of time needed for completion, and how the achievement of objectives will lead to improvement over existing conditions. Expected outcomes, not processes, are preferable when writing the statements.

As to the evaluation of an executive, both the document and the final appraisal should be the cooperative work of board, or board committee, and the administrator. This practice will do much to develop trust and understanding. The expertise of both will be utilized, with opportunities for improving performance increasing while reducing stress.

The process might begin with the party most knowledgeable about the executive's duties. Usually this will be the executive him- or herself. Noting each line-item in the position description, the executive can develop a preliminary set of objectives and standards. Some items in the description will have a single objective; others will have many. The final selection and wording will reflect the desires of both board and executive.

By relating the instrument to the position description, the executive will be accountable to an extent for institutional matters not exclusively dependent upon that person's actions. This is to be expected. Executives should be charged with leadership for the progress and viability of the institution. Maintaining a balanced budget, increasing physical plant capacity by a certain percentage, or reducing student attrition by a stipulated amount are examples of goals on which the executive's performance might be partly judged. Additionally, any standard of performance selected must be centered on the time period chosen for the evaluation. The level or degree of institutional progress expected will depend on the length of time selected.

After measures of evaluation and procedures have been developed, they should be accepted and followed by the full board. The chairperson should insist on that being done. It is not easy to satisfy seven or more different bosses at once, which a board could be to an executive if the members have not come to collective agreement about their expectations.

Constructing the Instrument

A practical beginning in objective evaluation is to construct a document in several columns. Responsibilities based on line-items in the person's job description are listed as separate headings. These statements are followed by statements of activities and expected performance in two columns. The final column, actual performance, remains blank until the end of the evaluation period.

When compiling a document for an executive's evaluation, the board might choose to have the activities prioritized according to their relative importance. Additionally, the people involved must agree on the level of achievement to be attained for completing the tasks and activities satisfactorily. Insofar as possible each activity should be written in measurable, results-oriented, quantifiable terms. Statements concentrated on outcome are often the most meaningful.

An executive will ordinarily have to document the performance achieved and share the facts with the board at the time of evaluation. The results might be used not only for making decisions about retention and compensation but also for revising the instrument and setting new objectives for the next succeeding period of evaluation. If desired, actual performance on each activity and that occurring overall can be rated on a scale of 1 to 5, low to high, with a mid-value representing satisfactory achievement.

Figure 8.1 illustrates the procedure. It contains part of an instrument suitable for evaluating a superintendent of schools during a particular fiscal year.

The observer will readily notice in Figure 8.1 the objectivity, the measurability, and the chances for institutional and managerial improvement by having specific leadership activities defined for the chief executive. The increased probability of obtaining a more accurate and factual evaluation of performance than would be possible by ordinary methods should also be apparent. For evidence, one can compare the previous example with its specificity and the type of

---

RESPONSIBILITY #1: Provide leadership for the system.

(A third column <u>Actual Performance</u> is to be added and filled in during the evaluation.)

<u>Activities</u>	<u>Desired Performance</u>
	Performance is satisfactory when:
1.1 Plan annual goals and objectives for the district.	1.1a Written goals and objectives for the district are given to the board by July.
	1.1b The annual goals relate to the board's long-range goals and are ratified with few changes.
1.2 Develop management skills among the principals.	1.2a He leads two sessions on Management for Results and one on goal-setting.
	1.2b The principals submit acceptable written objectives for their schools.

Figure 8.1 continued on following page.   ▼   ▼   ▼   ▼

Figure 8.1 Executive's Evaluation Instrument

RESPONSIBILITY #1: Provide leadership for the system
(continued)

<u>Activities</u>

<u>Desired
Performance</u>

1.5 Conduct planning sessions with the board.	1.5a He holds two orientation sessions for the new members. 1.5b He provides sufficient information to the board for analyzing the districts strengths and weaknesses. 1.5c He plans the annual retreat and leads discussion on mission and goals. 1.5d A majority of the board rate the session worthwhile.

RESPONSIBILITY #8: Direct the building program.

8.1 Identify needed facilities.	8.1a He submits course and enrollment projections for 5 years ahead. 8.1b He obtains approval from the state for the new facility.
8.6 Develop educational specifications for the facility.	8.6a Faculty, staff, and board are engaged in the planning. 8.6b A complete document is produced, specifying all room and space requirements.

Figure 8.1 (continued) Executive's Evaluation Instrument

instrument which seeks a rating on broadly inclusive statements, such as "He provides effective leadership for the school district." An individual's rating on this point could be more easily assigned than justified. Without the specifically stated guiding measures on an objective instrument, many of the executive's accomplishments throughout the year could be overlooked and left uncredited.

Objective methods of evaluation should be a welcome relief for persons concerned about the inadequacies of traits scales, the short-comings of ratings by subordinates, and the general lack of concern for measuring results based on facts. Boards that previously based evaluations on personal opinions and general impressions are likely to be most impressed when they observe evidence of all their executive has accomplished in a given period. The evaluators have to recognize achievements and cannot be blinded by some proclivity to remember only those things which went poorly or failed.

The method described certainly requires more time and effort than the simple check-off approach based on feelings prevailing at the moment. Much thought and planning must go into the instrument's development, and the review process can be tedious. Nonetheless, the results can be worth the effort. Even a consensus of members, when based on nonobjective criteria, assumption, or hunch, will seldom attain the level of reliability possible with a well-structured, objective appraisal instrument.

Writing the Contract

Whether or not to provide the executive officer with a multi-year contract seems to be a debatable issue among boards. Boards should recognize for a fact that many competent administrators will not accept a top position without the security of more than a one-year contract (wherever permitted). A principal reason is that a board's composition, hence its posture and expectations, can change abruptly. As a counter argument, the board loses the flexibility of replacing an executive who holds an extended contract. Actually, executives rarely become incompetent abruptly. A board can extend a multi-year contract with reasonable confidence by carefully screening candidates at the time of employment. The development at the outset of a complete instrument similar to the one described herein can reinforce that confidence. A n objectively structured instrument provides other advantages relative to the contract period. For one thing, the executive's record can be referred to yearly to assess performance longitudinally. The record will identify ineffectiveness, areas needing improving, indications of mismanagement or improper conduct, and instances of exemplary performance. Those indications are not likely to be so precisely evident in a subjective evaluation.

Chapter 9

Evaluating Board Performance

The honor, prestige, and gratification which serving on a board can produce comes most readily to those who feel good about their participation. Board service can also be of incalculable benefit to an important institution. Yet, not all members approach the duties conscientiously enough. Participation by some is perfunctory and inconsequential.

The duties can be highly demanding when approached with a sense of commitment. This fact should be realized before membership is accepted, and an awareness of it is a basic step toward exemplary participation. Effectiveness does not simply happen. A member becomes effective as a result of knowing the board's purpose and role, correctly interpreting the forces affecting educational strengths and, above all, taking conscientious interest in learning whatever is necessary to perform constructively. For many, firm dedication and unrelenting effort are the primary elements in the process.

Just as a board needs to be assured the school or college is being managed effectively, interested observers need assurance the board is striving to do its best. An attitude must prevail among the members which, first, acknowledges that performance can and should be improved and, second, represents a desire to know what to improve. An instrument of evaluation can provide the evidence sought, if the desire is present for developing a good one and putting it to use.

Acknowledging the Need

The failure of an educational board to perform at a reasonably high level of competence seems to result from inexperience and a low level of accountability. Inherent in this is a dependency of relationships. Very likely many more board members would attempt to improve and become expert in their work if they were held accountable through stricter methods of evaluation. Thorough reviews of a board's performance seldom occur, either individually or as a group. Neither is there a penalty of dismissal and loss of income for ineffectiveness similar to that which pertains in the private directorship. Furthermore, normal terminations and replacements in membership do not assure excellence in a board's composition. Experience and competence are sometimes sacrificed in the turnover. A semblance of accountability does exist at times of re-election and reappointment, although those exercises are often as much a test of political astuteness and popularity as they are indicators of anything else. However one accedes to membership has much less importance than the individual's qualifications and desire to do well in the office.

Because its affairs are conducted largely without external control, a board's power is almost absolute and potentially awesome. That this power has been more often properly used than abused or misused is undoubtedly true. There remains, nevertheless, a need for consummate integrity. No excuse can be accepted for not striving for excellence in performance. Having the will is preliminary to putting forth the effort.

The evaluation of a board, as with institutional evaluation and the appraisal of management, should be comprehensive. The instrument used should address areas of accomplishment and concern. Also, it should attempt to identify problems which need further attention by the members. Since no board is merely the sum of its parts, evaluations of members should be undertaken individually and collectively as a means of avoiding or controlling difficulties.

Both an absence of standards and the presence of low ones invite poor performance. A board seems more likely to think in terms of the quality of its work and to set positive goals when faced with periodic evaluations. The level of performance sought sets the stage for administrative action, with the manner of performance at the top being practically infectious within the institution.

Defining the Purpose

Excepting the occasional informal assessment, analyses of board performance seem to be woefully neglected. Systematic evaluation should be viewed as a vital activity, but apparently there is widespread fear the results of an evaluation will be more embarrassing to individuals than useful to the institution. Formal evaluation of the board can be equally as important as appraisals of employees. To deny that equality is to conclude, incorrectly, that the board has a less significant part than others in the institution's progress and well-being.

An evaluation strengthens operations. It delves into the past with an eye to the future. Properly done, the process results in the classification of behavior as either *adequate* or *needing improvement*. Whether dealing with members individually or the group as a unit makes no difference in this regard.

Planning a Self-Study

Formal evaluations of a board could be conducted by employees, outside consultants, or the members themselves. Some possibilities are more advantageous than others, and some should be avoided altogether under ordinary conditions.

Methods protecting the identity of individuals are preferable. Neither the persons being evaluated nor those doing the evaluating should be identifiable to others. To associate specifics with names and allow them to become public knowledge is to add still another negative to the reasons against serving on a board. Although the use of an outside consultant would naturally lead to some knowledge of the persons involved, a professional must hold an impersonal view of those evaluated and is duty-bound to maintain complete confidentiality.

Similar precautions should be exercised relative to assembling a group of citizens for the evaluation. Only rarely could such a body be expected to perform effectively. Few would have specific knowledge about the board and its interworkings, and the public's involvement in the board's assessment could lead to severe tensions. It might even do more harm than good. Ordinarily, the probable risk and problems would be too great to justify pursuing this course of action.

Neither are evaluations by employees recommended. The many reasons for avoiding assessments by subordinates apply here. The fact that national accrediting agencies accept and sometimes have encouraged such evaluations of boards and other superiors is not convincing evidence the practice should be duplicated. The process of accreditation necessarily requires internal evaluations that are not too negative, a matter which has probably influenced many a concerned employee. The importance of accreditation to the institution and the need to obtain reasonably favorable internal ratings to achieve that end are interrelated factors which must be acknowledged. Moreover, the problems mentioned in previous chapters about the involvement of subordinates are too important to be ignored for the purposes at hand.

Evaluation of the board by the person closest and most knowledgeable of the situation, the executive, also holds little merit. Lacking the protection of anonymity, the executive would have a particularly uneasy task to fulfill. This individual has the prodigious problem of trying to be openly honest while being aware that sincere truthfulness might create extreme difficulties in future personal and professional relations. Somewhat in the manner of a consultant, an executive could probably serve best by assisting the board in its planning for evaluation and by helping conduct reviews in a less formalized and diplomatic manner.

Structured self-evaluations seem to present the fewest drawbacks, despite their shortcomings. Inwardly directed analyses of members individually and as a group might not be as objective as evaluations from independent sources, but in the final analysis, persons in positions of leadership must learn to realize when one's own performance is effective. Participation in a self-study helps attain that end.

A self-study should be carefully planned. The executive with the aid of a consultant, if desired, can provide valuable suggestions. A committee of the board could do most of the work. Its assignment might include: (1) planning the process, (2) developing an instrument or instruments, (3) setting procedures for administering the evaluation, (4) tabulating results, and (5) scheduling a time and the process for reviewing findings. Decisions as to frequency, place, and content of the instrument remain subject to review and acceptance by the full board. All members should be present for the final discussion of results and techniques for improvement.

Evaluating One's Self

Attitudes, preparation, and participation ordinarily vary considerably among members. Even in a board that functions reasonably well, one or two members might carry the weight of responsibility. Inadequate performance by a single person detracts from the board's full potential. For that reason, it is advisable for every individual to evaluate his or her performance apart from the actions of others. One can scarcely expect the full board to be most effective if the members themselves make no effort to attain a high level of effectiveness.

Presented below are several questions to which individuals should seriously respond in a self-analysis. The questions are merely examples taken from the instrument presented in Appendix B. As in the complete instrument, the questions are separated into three categories. These are printed in italics. A scheme for scoring responses on a frequency scale is also presented with the instrument.

The examples included here and in the complete instrument should be reviewed and modified as appropriate before being adopted by the board.

Preparation. Questions in this category are posed relative to knowledge of board and institutional affairs, conscientiousness and thoroughness in acquiring an understanding of and performing responsibilities, and a desire to learn to be most effective in meetings throughout the term of office. An example: Can you explain the purpose and duties of the board?

Participation. The purpose here is to list questions that delve into the individual's actual performance, both during and outside meetings of the board. Formally assigned tasks, such as committee work, and the more casual or incidental associations with the constituency are legitimate areas about which to question a member's actions. How effectively a person performs will probably be reflected in the adequacy of his or her preparation. One such question might be: Do you present acceptable motions and recommendations for board action?

Relationships. How individuals deal with and react to persons on the board and within the institution is important for a smoothly operating organization. Inquiries about relations with the executive are needed, in particular. A broadly couched question in this area reads thus: Do you keep negative views of others out of the public arena?

In addition to the benefits to individuals, the board can profit from a summation of scores on all questionnaires. The completed instruments might be returned unsigned to the chief executive or committee chairperson for tabulating. Averages can then be calculated, either by section or by item. In that way, composite scores can be discussed at a session of the full board without revealing the identity of any one person.

Evaluating the Board

The process of evaluating performance by the board as a unit might not be enthusiastically received. Sometimes ignored, occasionally rejected, and seldom conscientiously applied, accountability in this matter has not been given the attention needed. There seems to be very limited understanding of how an evaluation of the board's performance can make much difference in the important issue of attaining educational results. Is it not the central objective of the institution to translate the talents and expertise of its staff and faculty into significant learning by students? Indeed it is. But to rationalize away the board's need for evaluating its actions is to fail to recognize the importance of accountability in leadership.

An apparent reason for little effort in this area is the work involved. An evaluation can be most effective if everyone is involved in developing criteria, rather than simply using externally prepared material as written. The process then proceeds from an analysis of duties and their implementation. The intellectual investment by individuals and the attempts to obtain agreement among the group can weigh heavily in time and effort.

In recognition of the potential problems, a board might profit by undertaking a study of a complete instrument. The one in Appendix C will serve as a guide. It contains 100 questions. The questions finally to be used, whether or not modified and adopted from those shown, could be duplicated as part of a survey for response by each member, with instructions clearly indicating the length of evaluation period covered.

The questions in the example ask individuals to respond not about their own preparation and participation but, instead, about how they perceive the board as a unit acts regarding different issues and concerns. The questions are grouped according to topics, as follows:

General Responsibility. This group of questions seeks to determine how effective the board is performing in different areas regarding learning and observing duties. How knowledgeable the board appears to be about institutional practices is an example.

Board Functioning. Questions about procedural matters in and out of meetings comprise this section.

Institutional Planning and Progress. Mission, purposes, and goals, particularly as regards the board's role, constitute this important area of questioning.

Relations with Management. Inquiries centered on the board's understanding of managerial duties and support of the executive are covered here.

Policy Determination. The practice and manner of policy setting are central to this section.

Performance Evaluation. Formal evaluation as it pertains to employees at all levels, in addition to the board's evaluation, is the subject of inquiry in this last topic.

When preparing questions about these topics, the chair should take the initiative. A committee might be assigned to the task, with the understanding of having its recommendations submitted to the full board for review and input. The duplication and administration of the instrument, including the collating of anonymous responses, could be assigned either to the chief executive or a committee. The results should be discussed in a post-evaluation conference. In fact, the exercise has little value unless the full board analyzes responses in the aggregate.

Striving for Improvement

The analysis and discussion of results can be handled efficiently by having a committee prepare a summary of results for consideration by the full membership. Areas of close agreement and those indicating sharp divergence of views should be singled out for special attention. A private session must be set aside for the discussion so that free interchange can occur.

Critical self-analysis should lead to recommendations for improvement, and the suggestions which emerge should be forthcoming in sufficient time to have an effect before the next evaluation. When coupled with the individual evaluations previously discussed, the results of a whole-board evaluation can be beneficial for all concerned.

Knowing When to Resign

There are valid reasons for resigning from a board. Important among them are those personal reasons which make continuation in service no longer possible or desirable. Problems pertaining to family, health, career, and values sometimes deserve *a priori* consideration. Nobody can be expected to attempt to render service gratuitously or with practically no compensation when faced with serious difficulties sometimes attendant to daily living. A person's first responsibility is to him- or herself and family, and nobody should attempt to shoulder the added burden of doing some other social good when utterly ineffective participation will be the likely result.

Other considerations may prevail, too. A member should terminate service on a board not only when lacking the time, ability, or interest to carry out duties but also when insupportable major differences in an organization's direction are advanced and continue beyond one's control. Resigning under such conditions could be the best thing to do. As a member's participation and influence approaches zero, the impact of that person's resignation on the organization also approaches zero.

Another general category of reasons for resigning prior to completing a term of office pertains to dysfunctional participation. Unlike the effects of nonparticipation, the results from this form of performance are obviously detrimental and often seriously counteractive. The possible adversities are manifold. Continually agitating and criticizing, instead of facilitating board and managerial actions, failing to follow protocol and other approved manners of conduct, and generally making uninformed, sometimes ludicrous proposals are several examples. The persistence and seriousness of any negative action should be weighed against anything the person does constructively before the chairperson decides to offer counsel in private. Allowed to continue unchecked, the negative actions of one can have a far-reaching impact

Counseling by the chairperson has been known to be very effective in obtaining a change of behavior and in prompting resignation. Conditions which might lead to the latter are summarized as follows:

1. When a member's special concern or self-interest is given precedence over the welfare of the institution and interests of constituents.

2. When legal, moral, or ethical requirements are being violated.

3. When the assignment is not taken seriously enough to learn what effective participation entails.

4. When the institution's mission and philosophy, consequently the institution itself, can no longer be supported in principle and rhetoric.

5. When maturity of judgment is missing so that major problems are created for the board, management, and the school or college's operational components.

6. When evaluations reveal performance is generally inadequate and does not improve.

7. When valid personal reasons, such as poor health, make the commitment an unreasonable burden.

Whatever the reasons for resigning, the need for persons who will perform duties by placing foremost the progress of the institution and its direction for social good still holds. A board not dominated by the positive actions of effective participants would be a pathetic body to behold.

Initial intentions might be entirely positive, but power tends to corrupt the ill-prepared. And that includes board members. This is not to say that they are inclined to do things illegally; simply, it is a firmly worded precaution against falling into the easy stance of a dictatorial authority. The legal authority vested in the board can be easily misconstrued by some to mean absolute authority. The result could be an abuse of power.

Commonly—too commonly perhaps—some persons seek membership on a board expressly for "making the people there shape-up," a situation akin to the posture of the "gunslinging" radical who joins the police force for the power and authority over people that the uniform and firearm provide. Self-evaluation is not likely to correct such deep-seated attitudes. Neither is it likely to cause resignation. It does, at least, direct the individual's attention to certain personal behaviors, and with adequate discussion and collective scrutiny, it holds out the prospect of good results—even in strongly negative cases.

Anyone considered worthy of appointment or election to a board has the potential to become an effective member. Paramount in the person's list of needs is a conscientious attitude. Next in line is to put forth an effort to follow positive recommendations such as outlined and detailed in this book. Resignation then need be a consideration only in rare, uncontrollable circumstances.

Appendix A

Criteria for Assessing a College's Strength

STUDENTS

1. Diversity of clientele
   - a. Part- and full-time student mix
   - b. Day versus evening enrollment
   - c. Age, sex, marital, ethnical mix
   - d. Distribution by programs of study
   - e. Employed versus unemployed students
   - f. Geographic distribution of clientele
   - g. Numbers dependent on financial aid
   - h. Standardized test performance
2. Enrollment trend/stability
   - a. Growth trend
   - b. Attrition
   - c. Seasonal variations
3. Constituency demand trend
   - a. New admissions versus total enrollment
   - b. Returning and transferring students comparison
   - c. Graduates versus terminators
   - d. Achievement of grads, state boards, etc.
4. Specialization
   - a. Technical course enrollment by proportion
   - b. Numbers in unique programs
   - c. Percentage in remedial programs

5. Market
   a. Available pool or prospects (potential market)
   b. Performance of competition
   c. Portion of market enrolled
   d. Marketing advantages and trends in the area
   e. Performance versus effort

SERVICES

1. Primary mission resource level
   a. Diversity of degree course offerings
   b. Provision of unique programs of study
   c. Technical education/liberal arts mix
   d. Relative credit/noncredit course effort
2. Secondary missions resource level
   a. Diversity of student activities
   b. Variety of intramural activities
   c. Variety of intercollegiate sports
   d. Counseling and advisement services
   e. Student employment opportunities
   f. Community and cultural services
3. Services Trend
   a. Interest demand versus new program offerings
   b. Growing versus declining offerings
   c. Income producing versus nonproductive services
   d. Instructional costs per student by program
   e. Non-instructional costs per student
   f. Program growth, stability, and deletion trends
   g. Special provisions, e.g., for senior citizens
4. Quality achievement
   a. Accreditation progress
   b. Results of evaluations
   c. Placement and goal achievement record
   d. Transferability of university parallel courses
   e. Community advisory support
5. Accessibility
   a. Ease of admissions versus selectivity
   b. Proximity of campus to clientele
   c. Off-campus offerings
   d. Provision of free parking
   e. Early admission, credit waiver opportunities
   f. Restrictions on services

FINANCES

1. Primary mission resource level
   a. Relative expenditures for instruction
   b. State subsidy for instruction
   c. Federal government support
   d. Local tax support
   e. Capital improvements funding
2. Secondary missions resource level
   a. Student aid support
   b. Student services support
   c. External support via gifts and donations
   d. Cultural and community services support
   e. Solvency of auxiliary enterprises
   f. Capital improvements funding
3. Capital resources trend
   a. Total income growth
   b. Freedom from deficit budgeting
   c. Comparative bond indebtedness
   d. Annual budget performance
4. Client and constituency support
   a. Relative dependence on tuition
   b. Changes in tuition and fee levels
   c. Charitable trust contributions
   d. Scholarship contributions
5. Fiscal flexibility
   a. Ratio of financial reserves to expenditures
   b. Percentage of unrestricted revenue
   c. Contingency reserves
   d. Cash flow (debt-equity) structure
   e. Investment and return on investments
   f. Ratio of fixed costs to total expenditures

FACILITIES

1. Primary mission resource level
   a. Plant space for instructional purposes
   b. Plant space for support services
   c. Equipment for instructional purposes
   d. Provisions for new needs and replacement

2. Secondary missions resource level
    a. Space for counseling, admissions, and testing
    b. Space for athletics and related activities
    c. Space for community and cultural uses
    d. Provisions for auxiliary enterprises
    e. Adequacy of equipment for secondary missions
3. Physical plant resources flexibility
    a. Availability of land for building expansion
    b. Room utilization per full-time students
    c. Off-campus rental needs and experience
    d. Contingency for maintenance and repairs
    e. Land holdings versus rental income
4. Plant condition and efficiency
    a. Maintenance costs versus total budget
    b. Operating costs in relation to total budget
    c. Environmental aesthetics
    d. Adequacy of unrestricted parking
    e. Energy conservation performance
5. Plant development trend
    a. Facilities construction pattern
    b. Capital improvement assets trend
    c. State support for building program
    d. Owned versus bonded and leased property
    e. External support for buildings and equipment

PERSONNEL

1. Primary mission resource level
    a. Full-time versus part-time faculty
    b. Qualifications of faculty
    c. Qualifications of instructional support staff
    d. Availability of fully qualified personnel
2. Secondary mission resource level
    a. Qualifications of non-instructional personnel
    b. Availability of fully qualified personnel
3. Productivity/work load
    a. Student-faculty ratios
    b. Student-counselor ratios
    c. Advisement and ancillary activities load
    d. Class size by institutional division

4. Employment trend/stability
    a. Freedom from retrenchment
    b. Terminations and resignations
    c. Promotions versus opportunities
    d. Growth pattern in different categories
    e. Comparative compensation
5. Professional development
    a. Professional improvement of personnel
    b. Investment in personnel improvement programs

MANAGEMENT/GOVERNANCE

1. Personnel
    a. Qualifications of administrative personnel
    b. Training in management principles
    c. Stability in office
    d. Staff development effort
2. Planning, organizing, and controlling
    a. Division of work responsibilities
    b. Policy determination
    c. Long-range and master planning
    d. Strategic unit planning
    e. Anticipatory planning versus performance
3. Internal governance
    a. Organization for participatory governance
    b. Controlling and evaluating performance
4. Institutional development trend
    a. Resource allocation for marketing
    b. Effective utilization of various resources
    c. Overall development of the institution
5. Organizational trend
    a. Structural changes versus overall growth
    b. Personnel development versus overall growth
6. Other criteria

RATING SCALE

5 ▸ Outstanding; performance substantially beyond need.
4 ▸ Above average; good, strong performance; no fault.
3 ▸ Average; adequate, competitive, solid performance.
2 ▸ Should be better; deteriorating; cause for concern.
1 ▸ Worrisome; must be improved; possible crisis; bad.

Appendix B

Board Member's Self-Evaluation

Instructions: Respond thoughtfully to all questions and place a numerical score after each. Compute average scores for each section and the total list when completed. Scoring: 5▸ Always or all, 4▸ Frequently or most, 3▸ Sometimes or some, 2▸ Seldom or few, 1▸ Never or none.

Preparation and Planning
1. Do you take your assignment on the board seriously?
2. Do you read all material distributed prior to meetings?
3. Do you read literature on board service which comes to your attention?
4. Are you prepared to ask relevant questions?
5. Are you prepared to discuss the major laws pertaining to board service and to the institution?
6. Are you able to give an adequate explanation of the institution's offerings when asked in the community?
7. Do you keep informed by attending meetings of your association, visiting other campuses, and talking to board members elsewhere?
8. Do you participate in special sessions and retreats when scheduled for the board?
9. Can you explain what your duties as a board member are?
10. Are you knowledgeable about board bylaws and policies?
11. Can you intelligently discuss the budget, student activities, and building plans?

12. Do you keep informed about trends that may affect your institution?
13. Do you enter meetings prepared to discuss institutional goals intelligently?
14. Can you recall the institution's long-range goals and plans?
15. Are you adequately versed in parliamentary procedure?
16. Do you think reflectively about meetings as a means of improving your future participation?

Participation
1. Do you attend regularly scheduled meetings?
2. Do you attend special meetings when scheduled?
3. Are you an active participant on committees?
4. Are you prompt to meetings?
5. Do you contribute constructively to board affairs?
6. Do you verbalize your thoughts on important issues?
7. Do you initiate recommendations and motions?
8. Are your recommendations accepted?
9. Do you ask insightful questions of staff when more information is needed for making decisions?
10. Do you consider it your duty to act in the interest of the institution, rather than some group?
11. Do you vote your conviction on important issues, without regard to the popularity of your decision?
12. Would you abstain from voting if there is a possibility of conflict of interest on your part?
13. Do you subordinate special or constituent interest to the institution's welfare?
14. Have you avoided becoming a "pipeline" for groups seeking attention by the board?
15. Do you support final decisions whether you agree with them or not?
16. Do you attend the institution's cultural and social events?
17. Do you confine your comments on board matters to board circles, unless authorized to act as spokesperson?

Relationships
1. Do you support the institution's mission?
2. Do you avoid arguments within the board?
3. Do you know what your executive's primary duties are?

4. Do you speak favorably about the institution and personnel in public?
5. Do you support and defend your executive officer?
6. Do you view your assignment primarily as a duty and not for the prestige it affords?
7. Would you prefer to represent this institution more than any other?
8. Do you politely and sincerely refuse to be the recipient of unfounded criticism about the institution?
9. Do you refer allegations about the executive to that person before taking any other action?
10. Do you allow administrators sufficient time to answer charges brought against them?
11. Are you observant of the chain of command when dealing with employees?
12. Do you know the difference between policy making and administration?
13. Do you attempt to influence legislators on relevant issues?
14. Do you work at gaining friends for the school in the community?
15. Do you work with, not around, your chairperson?
16. Speaking as chairperson, would you consider it your responsibility to talk seriously to a board member whose actions are dysfunctional?
17. Do you believe it is improper to influence selection of an employee by recommending a relative, friend, or acquaintance?

Appendix C

Board's Evaluation Instrument

Give your appraisal of how the board is performing by scoring each question as follows: 5▸ Excellent, 4▸ Good, 3▸ Fair, 2▸ Poor, and 1▸ Inadequate.

General Responsibility
1. Are board members knowledgeable about their duty?
2. Has the sunshine law been violated in any way?
3. Has the board written, reviewed, or revised a code of ethics for members?
4. Has any instance of conflict of interest occurred?
5. Has any effort at influence peddling been accepted?
6. Have members' job descriptions been written and reviewed?
7. Do committees and officers operate according to written job descriptions?
8. Do members avoid representing special interests?
9. Does the institution receive the full support of the board in the community?
10. Do members follow the chain of command in internal dealings?
11. Do members keep updated on relevant issues?
12. Does the board take a collective position and active stance on pertinent legislation?
13. Does the board demonstrate concern about the quality of instruction and learning above all else?

14. Do members come prepared to discuss the issues?
15. Do members attend seminars held by their association?
16. Did each member attend at least one school function during the past year?
17. Does the board work at gaining private support?

Board Functioning
1. Has the board given away any of its authority?
2. Does the chairperson control obstructionists and cliques?
3. Is the board strong enough to handle critics?
4. Is the board often divided over important issues?
5. Is the chairperson a leader and not simply a moderator?
6. Are all members kept involved in board activities?
7. Are meetings conducted in a businesslike manner?
8. Are spectators allowed to engage in discussions during meetings?
9. Have spectators been allowed to disrupt a meeting?
10. Are most recommendations by professionals accepted?
11. Has the board remained out of direct negotiations with faculty and other groups?
12. Does the chairperson resolve conflicts effectively?
13. Do all members observe the designated spokesperson's authority to speak on behalf of the board?
14. Have members demonstrated an awareness of how to address the chair and enter discussions?
15. Are meetings preplanned and efficiently conducted?
16. Is parliamentary procedure followed?
17. Are committees used effectively?
18. Does only the full board make policy decisions?
19. Does the board understand the institution and the trends that affect it?

Institutional Planning and Progress
1. Does the board periodically review institutional purposes and mission?
2. Does the board become engaged in goal setting?
3. Has the board held an annual planning retreat?
4. Is planning for the future a matter for the entire body?
5. Does the board do long-range planning annually?
6. Does the board require and participate in master planning for the institution?

7. Is an effort made to identify issues and problems several years ahead?
8. Are strategies developed for addressing possible contingencies?
9. Has the board evaluated institutional progress at least once during the past year?
10. Is the progress of the institution held uppermost?
11. Do members participate in planning sessions?
12. Does master planning proceed from an analysis of the institution's strengths and weaknesses?
13. Do the plans identify relationships between quality achievement and management, personnel, and services?
14. Is the board's effort adequate to obtain the necessary finances and facilities for the instructional program?
15. Is some part of each meeting set aside for considering the institution's future and planning for it?

Relations with Management
1. Do the executive and staff receive open support by the board?
2. Has management been actively supported in the face of some allegation or charge?
3. Is executive turnover too frequent in your institution?
4. Are employees allowed to by-pass the chain of command as a way to the board?
5. Do board committees avoid operating in administrative territory?
6. Is administration left to administrators by the board?
7. Is authority explicitly noted when delegated?
8. Are job descriptions required for all employees?
9. Are reports and discussions at meetings kept to the point?
10. Does the executive have freedom to lead and experiment?
11. Is management required to document its successes?
12. Does the board have a clear picture of employee performance?
13. Is the executive free to attend seminars, state and national events, etc.?
14. Is the approval of travel for employees left to administrative judgment?
15. Has an amount been budgeted for the year for travel to appropriate meetings by board members?
16. Has the executive been asked to identify areas which tend to hinder his or her actions?
17. Is the executive provided a multi-year contract?

18. Is management expected to write objectives measurably?
19. Does the board operate in a highly cooperative manner with the executive?

Policy Determination
1. Are all policies put into writing?
2. Has the difference between policy and administration ever been discussed formally?
3. Is the policy manual constructed for easy revision?
4. Have the policies been thoroughly reviewed or revised in the past two years?
5. Does the board make decisions only after examining alternatives?
6. Are affected constituencies consulted prior to policy adoption?
7. Does the board follow its policies and bylaws without exception?
8. Are policies adopted only a meeting or two after their official reading?
9. Have policies been implemented within the institution?
10. Have new members been oriented to board procedures?
11. Have policies and bylaws been adopted and revised according to set procedures?
12. Is the chief executive the only one permitted to make recommendations on behalf of employees?
13. Do members come prepared to offer alternatives to proposals?
14. Has the board adopted a policy covering evaluation of personnel, the institution, and itself?
15. Does the full board make final decisions on matters recommended by committees of members?

Performance Evaluation
1. Does the board evaluate the chief executive formally and objectively?
2. Is the chief executive provided an opportunity to suggest the method and content of his evaluation?
3. Does the board evaluate its performance annually?
4. Are post-evaluation reviews systematically conducted?
5. Are evaluations based on results as opposed to perceptions by subordinates?
6. Have evaluations of the board, either internally or by an outside agency, been predominately positive?

7. Does the board conduct evaluations so that performance can be improved?
8. Has the board's performance improved during the past several years?
9. Has the board ever acted against or criticized management without first having determined the facts?
10. Do members frequently ask questions which clearly hold faculty accountable for learning and student progress?
11. Does the executive know beforehand on what he will be evaluated?
12. Are evaluations by subordinates prohibited for purposes of promotion and retention?
13. Does the evaluation system place performance results above social relations criteria?
14. Is executive evaluation restricted to assessment by the board?
15. Does the chairperson prohibit the inclusion of rumor and allegation in the evaluation of management?

Index